Gaylord Watson

The United States of America

A Collection of Facts, Dates and Statistics

Gaylord Watson

The United States of America
A Collection of Facts, Dates and Statistics

ISBN/EAN: 9783337185800

Printed in Europe, USA, Canada, Australia, Japan

Cover: Foto ©Andreas Hilbeck / pixelio.de

More available books at **www.hansebooks.com**

UNITED STATES OF AMERICA,

A

COLLECTION OF FACTS, DATES
AND STATISTICS,

RESPECTING

THE GOVERNMENT, ARMY, NAVY, DIPLOMATIC RELATIONS, FINANCE
REVENUE, TARIFF, LAND SALES, HOMESTEAD AND NATURALIZA-
TION LAWS, DEBT, POPULATION OF THE UNITED STATES AND
EACH STATE AND CONSIDERABLE CITY, AGRICULTURAL
CONDITION, AREA FOR CULTIVATION, FOREIGN COINS
AND THEIR VALUE, EDUCATION AND RAILWAYS,
ETC., ETC.

BEING

THE MOST COMPLETE COLLECTION OF STATISTICS EVER
BROUGHT TOGETHER IN A SINGLE VOLUME
OF SMALL SIZE.

TO BE PRESENTED TO EACH PURCHASER OF

Watson's New Map of the United States.

NEW YORK:
GAYLORD WATSON,
16 BEEKMAN STREET.
1872.

WATSON'S NEW MAP OF THE UNITED STATES.

It has been our object in preparing this little manual, to furnish all without additional cost to you, though at heavy expense to ourselves, those general statistics which are likely to be wanted by a map purchaser. We think that we have succeeded in giving you the most valuable collection ever made in any moderate compass, and shall be greatly disappointed, if this does not largely increase the demand for our beautiful map. If the purchasers are satisfied with our effort to give them their money's worth, we shall be thoroughly content.

THE PUBLISHER.

THE GENERAL GOVERNMENT,

ITS PRINCIPAL DEPARTMENTS, OFFICERS OF THE CABINET, THE ARMY AND NAVY, AND THEIR SUBORDINATES—DIPLOMATIC RELATIONS—OUR MINISTERS AND CONSULS TO FOREIGN COUNTRIES, AND THEIRS TO THIS COUNTRY.

UNITED STATES GOVERNMENT.

PRESIDENT.

ULYSSES S. GRANT, of Galena, Illinois.   Term expires March 4, 1873.

The President is chosen by Electors, who are elected by the People, each State having as many as it has Senators and Representatives in Congress.   He holds office four years; is Commander-in-Chief of the Army and Navy of the United States; has power to grant pardons and reprieves for offenses against the United States; makes treaties, by and with the advice and consent of the Senate; nominates, and, with the consent of the Senate, appoints, all Cabinet, Diplomatic, Judicial and Executive officers; has power to convene Congress, or the Senate only; communicates with Congress by message at every session; receives all Foreign Ministers; takes care that the laws are faithfully executed, and the public business transacted.   Salary $25,000 a year.

VICE-PRESIDENT.

SCHUYLER COLFAX, of South Bend, Ind.   Term expires March 4, 1873.

Is chosen by the Electors at the same time, and in the same manner as the President; is President of the Senate, and has the casting vote therein.   In case of the death, resignation, disability or removal of the President, his powers and duties devolve upon the Vice-President for the residue of his term.   In cases of vacancy, where the Vice-President succeeds to the Presidential office, the President of the Senate becomes *ex officio* Vice-President.   Salary, $8,000 a year.

THE STATE DEPARTMENT

Preserves the public archives, records, laws, documents and treaties, and supervises their publication; conducts all business and correspondence arising out of Foreign Relations; makes out and records passports, commissions, etc.

Department Officers.

Secretary of State: Hamilton Fish, of New York.
Assistant Secretary:*   Vacant for the term.
Second Assistant Secretary: Wm. Hunter, of Rhode Island.

* Mr. Davis is now of the Counsel for the Government before the International Board of Arbitrators at Geneva, Switzerland.

Diplomatic Officers.

COUNTRY.	NAMES.	OFFICE.	FOREIGN RESIDENCE.	STATE FROM.
Great Britain	Robert C. Schenck	Minister	London	Ohio.
do	Benjamin Moran	Sec. Leg.	do	Pennsylvania.
do	M. Woodhull	Asst. Sec.	do	
do	Adam Badeau	Con.-Gen.	do	New York.
do	Thomas H. Dudley	Consul	Liverpool	New Jersey.
do	Isaac Jenkinson	do	Glasgow	Indiana.
do	James Rea	do	Belfast.	Illinois.
East Indies	A. C. Litchfield	Con.-Gen.	Calcutta	Michigan.
Australia	Thomas Adamson, Jr.	Consul	Melbourne	West Virginia.
Canada	Wm. A. Dart	Con.-Gen.	Montreal	New York.
Russia	Andrew G. Curtin	Minister	St. Petersburg	Pennsylvania.
do	Eugene Schuyler	Sec. Leg.	do	New York.
do	George Pomutz	Consul	do	Iowa.
do	S. P. Young	Vice-Con.	Moscow	Illinois.
France	Elihu B. Washburne	Minister	Paris	Illinois.
do	Wickham Hoffman	Sec. Leg.	do	Louisiana.
do	Frank Moore	Asst. Sec.	do	New York.
do	S. L. Glasgow	Consul	Havre	Iowa.
do	Milton M. Price	do	Marseilles	Iowa.
Spain	Daniel E. Sickles	Minister	Madrid	New York.
do	Alvey A. Adee	Sec. Leg.	do	New York.
do	Alfred S. Duffie	Consul	Cadiz	Rhode Island.
Cuba	Alfred T. A. Torbert	Con.-Gen.	Havana	Delaware.
Portugal	Charles H. Lewis	Minister	Lisbon	Virginia.
do	Vacant	Sec. Leg.	do	
do	Henry W. Diman	Consul	do	Rhode Island.
do	James C. Fletcher	do	Oporto	Indiana.
Belgium	J. R. Jones	Minister	Brussels	Illinois.
do	Vacant	Sec. Leg.	do	
do	Aug. L. Chetlain	Consul	do	Utah.
do	James R. Weaver	do	Antwerp	West Virginia.
Netherlands	Charles I. Gorham	Minister	The Hague	Michigan.
do	Frederick Schuts	Consul	Rotterdam	New York.
do	Charles Mueller	do	Amsterdam	Ohio.
Denmark	M. J. Cramer	Minister	Copenhagen	Kentucky.
Sweden & Norway	C. C. Andrews	do	Stockholm	Minnesota.
do do	F. K. Bazier	Consul	Gottenburg	New Jersey.
Prussia	George Bancroft	Minister	Berlin	New York.
do	Alexander Bliss	Sec. Leg.	do	New York.
do	Nicholas Fish	Asst. Sec.	do	
do	William P. Webster	Con.-Gen.	Frankfort	Massachusetts.
Saxony	John H. Stewart	Consul	Leipsic	Pennsylvania.
Bremen	Robert M. Hanson	do	Bremen	Ohio.
Hamburg	Edward Robinson	do	Hamburg	New York.
Bavaria	G. Henry Horstman	do	Munich	Pennsylvania.
Wurtemberg	E. Klauprecht	do	Stuttgart	Ohio.
Baden	William H. Young	do	Carlsruhe	Ohio.
Hesse Darmstadt	Aaron Seeley	do	Darmstadt	New York.
Austria	John Jay	Minister	Vienna	New York.
do	John P. Delaplaine	Sec. Leg.	do	New York.
do	P. Sidney Post	Consul	do	Illinois.
Switzerland	Horace Rublee	Minister	Berne	Wisconsin.
do	Henry Erni	Consul	Basle	Tennessee.
do	Charles H. Upton	do	Geneva	Virginia.
Italy	George P. Marsh	Minister	Rome	Vermont.
do	George W. Wurts	Sec. Leg.	do	
do	David M. Armstrong	Con.-Gen.	do	New York.
do	O. M. Spencer	Consul	Genoa	Iowa.
do	B. Odell Duncan	do	Naples	South Carolina.
Papal Dominion	David M. Armstrong	do	Rome	New York.
Turkey	George H. Boker	Minister	Constantinople	New York.
do	John P. Brown	Sec. Leg.	do	Ohio.
do	J. H. Goodenow	Con.-Gen.	do	Maine.
do	R. Beardsley	Consul	Jerusalem	Indiana.
Egypt	G. H. Butler	Con.-Gen.	Alexandria	California.
do	Victor Barthow	Consul	Cairo	
Greece	John M. Francis	Minister	Athens	New York.
Barbary States	F. A. Matthews	Consul	Tangier	California.
Liberia	J. W. Mason	Minister	Monrovia	Arkansas.
Muscat	John F. Webb	Consul	Zanzibar	Massachusetts.
Madagascar	J. P. Finkel Meier	Com. Agt.	Tamatave	New Jersey.
Japan	C. E. De Long	Minister	Yeddo	
do	A. L. C. Portman	Interpreter	do	New York.
do	Charles O. Shepard	Consul	Kanagawa	New York.
Siam	F. W. Partridge	do	Bangkok	Illinois.
China	Frederick F. Low	Minister	Peking	California.
do	S. Wells Williams	Sec. Leg.	do	New York.
do	George F. Seward	Con.-Gen.	Shanghai	New York.
do	Vacant	Consul	Canton	
do	Milton M. De Lano	do	Foo Chow	California.

Diplomatic Officers—(Continued.)

COUNTRY.	NAMES.	OFFICE.	FOREIGN RESIDENCE	STATE FROM.
Hawaiian Islands	Henry A. Pierce	Minister	Honolulu	Massachusetts.
do do	Calvin S Mattoon	Consul	do	Ohio.
do do	H. H. Houghton	do	Lahaina	Illinois.
Hayti	E. D. Bassett	Minister	Port au Prince	Pennsylvania.
San Domingo	Fisher W. Ames	Com. Agt	St. Domingo	Ohio.
Mexico	Thomas H. Nelson	Minister	Mexico	Kentucky.
do	Porter C. Bliss	Sec. Leg.	do	Dis't Columbia.
do	Henry A. Badham	Con.-Gen.	Tampico	North Carolina.
do	Julius A. Skilton	Consul	Mexico	Louisiana
do	Thomas F. Wilson	do	Matamoras	Pennsylvania.
do	S. S. Trowbridge	do	Vera Cruz	Illinois.
Nicaragua	Charles N. Riotte	Minister	Nicaragua	
do	B. Squire Cotrell	Com. Agt	San Juan Del Norte	New York.
do	Rufus Mead	Consul	San Juan Del Sur	Vermont.
Costa Rica	Jacob B. Blair	Minister	San Jose	West Virginia.
Guatemala	S. A. Hudson	do	Guatemala	Iowa.
do	Henry Honben	Consul	do	
Honduras	Henry Baxter	Minister	Comayagua	Michigan.
Salvador	Thomas Biddle	do	San Salvador	Pennsylvania.
Colombia	S. A. Hurlbut	do	Bogota	Illinois.
do	Owen M. Long	Consul	Panama	Illinois.
do	Charles E. Perry	do	Aspinwall	New York.
Venezuela	William A. Pile	Minister	Caraccas	Missouri.
do	Charles H. Loehr	Consul	Laguayra	Pennsylvania.
Ecuador	E. Rumsey Wing	Minister	Quito	Kentucky.
do	Charles Weile	Consul	Guayaquil	Nevada.
Brazil	James R. Partridge	Minister	Rio de Janeiro	Maryland.
do	Richard C. Shannon	Sec. Leg.	do do	
do	Datus E. Coon	Consul	do do	Alabama.
do	Joseph Stryker	do	Pernambuco	Maine.
Argentine Conf.	Robert C. Kirk	Minister	Buenos Ayres	Ohio.
do do	Dexter E. Clapp	Consul	do do	New York.
Paraguay	John L. Stevens	Minister	Asuncion	Maine.
do	Vacant	Consul	do	
Chili	Joseph P. Root	Minister	Santiago	Kansas.
do	John C. Caldwell	Consul	Valparaiso	Maine.
Peru	Thomas Settle	Minister	Lima	North Carolina
do	H. M. Brent	Sec. Leg	do	California.
do	D. J. Williamson	Consul	Callao	California.
Bolivia	Leopold Markbreit	Minister	La Paz	Ohio.

FOREIGN LEGATIONS IN THE UNITED STATES.

Argentine Republic—Senor Don Manuel R. Garcia, Envoy Ex. and Min. Plen.; —— —— Secretary of Legation.

Austria—Baron Charles Lederer, Envoy Ex. and Min. Plen.; Count M. Esterhazy, Attache.

Belgium—Mr. Maurice Delfosse, Minister Resident; Mr. Alfred Berghmans, Secretary of Legation.

Brazil—Senhor Dom Domingo Jose Gonsalves de Magalhaens, Envoy Ex. and Min. Plen.; Senhor Don Luis A. De Padua Fleury, Secretary ad interim.

Chili—Senor Don Joaquin Fleury, Envoy Ex. and Min. Plen.

Colombia—Senor Don Santiago Perez, Minister Resident; Senor Enrique Cortes, Secretary of Legation.

Costa Rica—Vacant.

Denmark—F. E. de Bille, Minister Resident. Absent. F. Christensen, Charge d' Affaires.

Ecuador—Senor Don Antonio Flores, Minister Resident.

France—M. le Viscount Jules Treilhart, Envoy Ex. and Min. Plen.; M. de Bellonnet, First Secretary of Legation; Mr. Paul Derjardin, Honorary Consul.

FOREIGN LEGATIONS IN THE UNITED STATES—(Continued.)

Great Britain—Edward Thornton, Esq., C. B., Envoy Ex. and Min. Plen.; Hon. T. J. Pakenham, First Secretary of Legation.

Greece—Mr. D. P. Botassi, Charge d' Affaires, *ad interim.*

Hayti—Mr. Stephen Preston, Minister Resident.

Hawaiian Islands—Mr. E. H. Allen, Envoy Ex. and Min. Plen.

Honduras—S. W. Odell, Charge d' Affaires, *ad interim.*

Italy—Count Luigi Corti, Envoy Ex. and Min. Plen.; Count Luigi Colbiano, Secretary of Legation.

Japan—Jugoi Arinori Mori, Charge d' Affaires; Masakazah Toyama, Secretary.

Liberia—Mr. Henry F. Schieffelin, Charge d' Affaires. William Coppinger, Secretary of Legation.

Mexico—Francisco G. Palacio, Charge d' Affaires, *ad interim ;* Cayetano Romero, First Secretary.

North German Union—Prussia—Mr. Schlozer, Envoy Ex. and Min. Plen.; Baron Alvensleben, Secretary of Legation.

Netherlands—Mr. H. Westenberg, Minister Resident.

Nicaragua—Senor Don Jose R. Perez, Charge d' Affaires.

Portugal—Chevalier de Sanza Lobo. Envoy Ex. and Min. Plen; Senhor Antonio Da Cunha, Secretary.

Peru—Colonel Don Manuel Freyre, Envoy Ex. and Min. Plen.; Don Eduardo Villena, Secretary.

Russia—Mr. Borris Danzas, *ad interim*, First Secretary of Legation; General Alexander Gorlow, Military Attache.

Spain—Senor Don Mauricio Lopez Roberts, Envoy Ex. and Min. Plen.; Senor Don Luis de Potestad, First Secretary of Legation.

Sweden and Norway—Mr. Oluf Stenersen, Envoy Ex. and Min. Plen.; Mr. E. de Cederstrahle, Secretary of Legation.

Salvador and Guatemala—Senor Jose Maria Vela, Charge d' Affaires.

Switzerland—Mr. John Hitz, Consul General; Mr. C. J. Ost, Sec'y.

Turkey—Blacque Bey, Envoy Ex. and Min Plen. ; Baltazzi Effendi, Secretary.

THE TREASURY DEPARTMENT

Receives and has charge of all moneys paid into the United States Treasury, has general supervision of the fiscal transactions of the Government, the collection of revenue, the auditing and payment of accounts and other disbursements, supervises the execution of the laws relating to Commerce and Navigation of the United States, the Revenues and Currency, the Coast Survey, the Mint and Coinage. the Light-House Establishment, the construction of Marine Hospitals, Custom-Houses, etc. The First Comptroller prescribes the mode of keeping and rendering accounts for the civil and diplomatic service, and the public land. To him the First, Fifth, and Sixth Auditors report. The Second Comptroller pre-

THE TREASURY DEPARTMENT—(Continued.)

scribes the mode of keeping and rendering accounts for the army, navy and Indian Departments, and to him the Second, Third and Fourth Auditors report. The First Auditor adjusts the accounts of the customs, revenue, civil service and private acts of Congress. The Second Auditor adjusts accounts relating to pay, clothing and recruiting of the army, the arsenals, armories and ordnance, and the Indian department. The Third Auditor adjusts accounts for army subsistence, fortifications, military academy and roads, quartermaster's department and military claims. The Fourth Auditor adjusts the navy accounts, the Fifth diplomatic, and the Sixth postal affairs.

Department Officers.

Secretary of the Treasury : George S. Boutwell, of Massachusetts.
Assistant Secretaries : Wm. A. Richardson, of Massachusetts.
John F. Hartley, of Maine.

WAR DEPARTMENT

Has charge of business growing out of military affairs, keeps the records of the army, issues commissions, directs the movement of troops, superintends their payment, stores, clothing, arms and equipments and ordnance, constructs fortifications, and conducts works of military engineering.

Department Officers.

Secretary of War: William G. Belknap, of Iowa.
Inspector General: Brevet Major General Edmond Schriver, of New York.
Judge Advocate General: Colonel Joseph Holt, of Kentucky.
Adjutant General: Brevet Major General E. D. Townsend, of District of Columbia.
Quartermaster General: Brevet Major General M. C. Meigs, of Pennsylvania.
Commissary General: Brevet Major General Amos B. Eaton, of New York.
Surgeon General: Brevet Major General Joseph K. Barnes, of Pennsylvania.
Paymaster General: Brevet Major General B. W. Brice, of Ohio.

General Officers of Regular Army.

NAME AND RANK.	ENTRY INTO SERVICE.	APPOINTED FROM.	NAME AND RANK.	ENTRY INTO SERVICE.	APPOINTED FROM.
General.			*Retired List.*		
Wm. T. Sherman ...	July 1, 1840	Ohio.	*Major Generals.*		
Lieutenant-General			Joseph Hooker......	July 1, 1837	California.
Philip H. Sheridan .	July 1, 1853	Ohio.	S. P. Heintzelman...	July 1, 1822	Penn.
Major-Generals.			Thomas J. Wood....	July 1, 1841	Kentucky.
			John C. Robinson ...	Ap'l 28, 1862	New York.
George G. Meade ...	July 1, 1835	Dis't Col.	Daniel E. Sickles....	Nov 29, 1862	New York.
Winfield S. Hancock.	July 1, 1844	Penna.	Samuel S. Carroll ...	July,—1852	Dis't Col.
John M. Schofield ..	July 1, 1837	California.	Thomas W. Sherman	July,—1832	R. Island.
Brigadier-Generals.			Richard W. Johnson	July,—1844	Kentucky.
			James B. Ricketts ...	Sept.—1835	New York.
Irwin McDowell....	July 1, 1838	Ohio.	Eli Long		
Philip St. G. Cooke..	July 1, 1827	Virginia.	*Brigadier-Generals.*		
John Pope	July 1, 1842	Illinois.	Gabriel R. Paul	July,—1729	Missouri.
Oliver O. Howard ...	July 1, 1854	Maine.	Francis Fessenden..	1862	Maine.
Alfred H. Terry	Jan 15, 1865	Conn.	William F. Lynch ...		
Edward O. C. Ord ..	July 1, 1839	Maryland.	Thomas W. Sweeney	Nov.—1862	New York.
Edward R. S. Canby	July 1, 1839	Kentucky.	Joseph B. Kiddlo....		
Christopher C. Augur	July 1, 1843	New York.	Martin D. Hardin...	July,—1834	Illinois.
			William S. Harney...	Feb.—1818	Louisiana.
			George D. Ramsay ..	Aug.—1814	Dis't Col.
			Richard Delafield ...	May,—1814	New York.
			L. Thomas	Sept.—1819	Delaware.

Commanders of Military Divisions and Departments.

DIVISIONS.	DEPARTMENTS.	STATES.	COMMANDERS.	HEADQUARTERS.
Of the Missouri			Lieut-Gen. P. H. Sheridan..	St. Louis, Mo.
	The Missouri.	Missouri, Kansas. Indian Territory Colorado, New Mexico, Illinois, Fort Smith, Arkansas	Maj. Gen. John Pope......	Ft Leavenworth
	The Platte..	Iowa, Nebraska, Utah, Wyoming,	Brev. Maj.-Gen. E. O. C. Ord	Omaha, Neb.
	Dakota	Minnesota. Dakota and Montana	Maj.-Gen. W. S. Hancock..	St. Paul's, Minn.
	Texas........		Brev. Maj.-Gen. C. C. Augur	San Antonio, Tex
Of the Pacific..	California	California, Nevada	Maj.-Gen. J. M. Schofield...	San Francisco.
	Columbia	Oregon, Washington Territory, Idaho and Alaska Territory ...		San Francisco.
	Arizona......	Arizona and California, south of a line from N. W. corner of Arizona to Point Conception	Brev.Maj.Gen.E.R.S.Canby Lieut. Col. George Cook....	Portland, O'gon. Prescott. Ariz.
Of the Atlantic	The East......	New England States, New York, New Jersey, Pennsylvania, Delaware, West Virginia, North Carolina, District of Columbia	Maj.-Gen. George G. Meade Brev. Maj.-Gen. McDowell	Philadelphia. N. Y. City.
	The Lakes...	Ohio, Michigan, Wisconsin, Indiana, and the frontier east to Lake Champlain	Brev.Maj.Gen.P.St.G.Cooke	Detroit, Mich.

NAVY DEPARTMENT

Has charge of the Naval Establishment and all business connected therewith, issues Naval Commissions, instructions and orders, supervises the enlistment and discharge of seamen, the Marine Corps, the construction of Navy Yards and Docks, the construction and equipment of Vessels, the purchase of provisions, stores, clothing and ordnance, the conduct of surveys and hydrographical operations.

Department Officer.

Secretary of the Navy : George M. Robeson, of New Jersey.

Officers of the Navy.

NAME AND RANK.	STATE FROM.	ENTRY INTO SERVICE.	NAME AND RANK.	STATE FROM.	ENTRY INTO SERVICE.
			Rear Admirals. Active List.		
Admiral.			William Radford ..	Mo......	March 1, 1825
David D. Porter	Pa	Feb. 2, 1829	Joseph Lanman	Conn ..	Jan. 21, 1825
Vice-Admiral.			John Rodgers	Md	April 18, 1828
Stephen C. Rowan ..	Ohio	Feb. 1, 1826	John A. Winslow ...	Mass ..	Feb. 1, 1837
			Samuel Phillips Lee	Va	July 17, 1862
Rear Admirals. Active List.			Oliver S. Glisson ...	Md...	July 17, 1862
			Melancthon Smith...	N. Y...	July 17, 1862
L. M. Goldsborough.	Md	June 18, 1812	Charles S. Boggs....	N. J...	July 17, 1862
Charles H. Davis....	Mass..	Aug. 12, 1823	Henry Walke	Ohio ..	July 17, 1862
Sylvanus W. Godon.	Pa	March 1, 1819	Thorn. A. Jenkins	Mass	July 17, 1862

Officers of the Navy—(Continued.)

NAME AND RANK.	STATE FROM.	ENTRY INTO SERVICE.	NAME AND RANK.	STATE FROM.	ENTRY INTO SERVICE.
Active List, Commodores.			*Active List, Commodores.*		
			Gustavus H. Scott..	Ind	Aug. 1, 1828
Wm. Rogers Taylor.	R. I.....	July 17, 1862	David McDougal ..	Cal	Sept. 1, 1823
Benjamin F. Sands..	Ky......	July 17, 1862	John J. Almy......	N. Y ...	Feb. 2, 1822
Charles Steedman ..	S. C	July 17, 1862	James H. Strong...	N. Y ...	Feb. 2, 1828
James Alden	Me	July 17, 1862	James M. Frailey...	Pa	May 1, 1828
Alfred Taylor	Va.	Jan. 1, 1825	Enoch G. Parrott ...	N. H ...	Dec. 16, 1831
Theodore P. Green ..		Nov. 1, 1862	Wm. Reynolds	Pa	Nov. 17, 1831
Joseph F. Green	Me	Nov. 1, 1827	Fabius Stanley	Cal......	Dec. 20, 1831
Augustus L. Case...	N. Y	April 1, 1828	Wm. H. Macomb ...	N. J. ...	April 10, 1834
Alex.r M. Pennock..	N. Y	Jan 10, 1834	Wm. E. LeRoy......	N. Y ...	Jan. 11, 1832
John L. Worden	N. Y	April 1, 1828	J. R. M. Mullany....	N. Y....	Jan. 7, 1832
Geo. F. Emmons	Vt	April 1, 1828	Roger N. Stembel...	Ohio	Mar. 27, 1832
Edward Middleton..	Cal	July 1, 1828	C. R. P. Rodgers...	N. J.....	Oct. 5, 1833

DEPARTMENT OF THE INTERIOR

Has charge of the survey, management, sales and grants of Public Lands, the examinations of Pension and Bounty Land claims, the management of Indian affairs, the examination of Inventions and award of Patents, the collection of statistics, the distribution of Seeds, Plants, etc. the taking of Censuses, the management of Government mines, the erection of Public Buildings, and the construction of wagon roads to the Pacific.

Department Officers.

Secretary of the Interior : Columbus Delano, of Ohio.
Assistant Secretary : Wm. T. Otto, of Indiana.

POST-OFFICE DEPARTMENT

Has charge of the Postal System, the establishment and discontinuance of Post-Offices, appointment of Postmasters, the contracts for carrying the mails, the Dead Letter Office, maintains an inspection to prevent frauds, mail depredations, etc.

Department Officers.

Postmaster-General : John A. J. Creswell, of Maryland.
Appointment Office, 1st Asst. P. M. General: J. W. Marshall, of Md.
Contract Office, 2d Asst. P. M. General : George A. Smith, of Ill.
Finance Office, 3d Asst. P. M. General : Wm. H. H. Terrill, of Ind.

DEPARTMENT OF JUSTICE.

The Attorney-General, who is the head of this department, is the legal adviser of the President and heads of departments, examines titles, applications for pardons, and judicial and legal appointments, conducts and argues suits in which Government is concerned, etc.

Department Officers.

Attorney-General : Amos T. Akerman, of Georgia.
Assistant Attorney-General : Clement H. Hill, of Massachusetts.
    do   do   Thomas H. Talbot, of Maine.
Solicitor General : B. H. Bristow, of Kentucky.

THE JUDICIARY.

Supreme Court of the United States.

APPOINTED.		AGES.	SALARY.
1862.	Salmon P. Chase, Ohio, *Chief Justice,*	63	$6,500
1845.	Samuel Nelson, Cooperstown, N. Y., *Asso. Jus.*	78	6,000
1858.	Nathan Clifford, Portland, Maine, do	67	6,000
1862.	Noah H. Swayne, Columbus, Ohio, do	61	6,000
1862.	David Davis, Bloomington, Illinois, do	56	6,000
1862.	Samuel F. Miller, Keokuk, Iowa, do	55	6.000
1863.	Stephen J. Field, California, do	54	6,000
1870.	John V. P. Bradley, New Jersey, do	58	6,000
1870.	William Strong, Pennsylvania, do	62	6,000

The Court holds one general term, annually, at Washington, D. C., commencing on the first Monday in December.

D. Wesley Middleton, of Washington, *Clerk.*
John M. Wallace, of Pennsylvania, *Reporter.*
Richard C. Parsons, of Ohio, *Marshal.*

Circuit Judges of the United States.

First Circuit—(Maine, New Hampshire, Vermont, Massachusetts, Rhode Island and Connecticut)—Geo. P. Shepley, of Portland, Maine.

Second Circuit—(New York)—Lewis B. Woodruff, of New York City.

Third Circuit—(Pennsylvania, New Jersey, Delaware, Maryland and Virginia)—William McKennan, of Pennsylvania.

Fourth Circuit—(North Carolina, South Carolina, Georgia, Florida, Alabama and Tennessee)—Hugh L. Bond, of Maryland.

Fifth Circuit—(Mississippi, Louisiana, Arkansas and Texas)—William B. Woods, of Alabama.

Sixth Circuit—(Ohio, Michigan, Kentucky and West Virginia)—Halmar H. Emmons, of Detroit, Michigan.

Seventh Circuit—(Indiana, Illinois and Wisconsin)—Thomas Drummond, of Chicago, Illinois.

Eighth Circuit—(Minnesota, Iowa, Missouri, Kansas and Nebraska)—John F. Dillon, of Dubuque, Iowa.

Ninth Circuit—(California, Oregon and Nevada)—Lorenzo Sawyer, of San Francisco.

District Courts—Judges. (States.)

Alabama, Richard Busteed. Arkansas, Henry C. Caldwell. California, Ogden Hoffman. Connecticut, Wm. D. Shipman. Delaware, Willard Hall. Florida, N. D., Philip Frazer. Florida, S. D., John M. McKinney. Georgia, John Erskine. Illinois, N. D., Henry W. Blodgett. Illinois, S. D., Samuel H. Treat, Jr. Indiana, Walter Q. Gresham. Iowa, James M. Love. Kansas, Mark W. Delahay. Kentucky, Bland Ballard. Louisiana, Edward H. Durell. Maine, Edward Fox. Mary-

District Courts—Judges. States. (Continued.)

land, William F. Giles. Massachusetts, John Lowell. Michigan, E. D., John M. Longyear. Michigan, W. D., S. L. Withey. Minnesota, R. R., Nelson. Mississippi, N. D., Robert A. Hill. Mississippi, S. D., Robert A. Hill. Missouri, E. D., Samuel Treat. Missouri, W. D., Arnold Krekel. Nebraska, Elmer S. Dundy. Nevada, Edgar W. Hillyer. New Hampshire, Daniel Clarke. New Jersey, John T. Nixon. New York, N. D., Nathan K. Hall. New York, S. D., Samuel Blatchford. New York, E. D., Charles L. Benedict. North Carolina, George W. Brooks. Ohio, S. D., Humph. H. Leavitt. Ohio, N. D , Charles T. Sherman. Oregon, Matthew P. Deady. Pennsylvania, E. D., John Cadwallader. Pennsylvania, W. D., Wilson McCandless. Rhode Island, John P. Knowles. South Carolina, George S. Bryan. Tennessee, Conolly F. Trigg. Texas, E. D., Joel C. C. Winch. Texas, W. D., T. H. Duval. Vermont, D. A. Smalley. Virginia, John C. Underwood. West Virginia, John J. Jackson. Wisconsin, E. D., Andrew G. Miller. Wisconsin, W. D., James G. Hopkins.

District Courts—Judges. (Territories.)

Arizona, John Titus. Colorado, Moses Hallett. Dakota, George W. French. Idaho, David Noggle. Montana, Henry L. Warren. New Mexico, Joseph G. Palin. Utah, James B. McKean. Washington, Owen Jacobs. Wyoming, John H. Howe. Dis't of Columbia, David K. Cartter, Wm. Humphreys, Abram B. Olin, Andrew Wylie, Arthur McArthur.

DEPARTMENT OF AGRICULTURE.

Commissioner of Agriculture : Horace Capron, of Connecticut.
Chief Clerk : R. T. McLain, of Ohio.
Chief of Correspondence : E. W. Whitaker of New York.
Statistical Clerk : J. R. Dodge, of Ohio.
Entomologist : Townend Glover, of Maryland.
Chemist : Thomas Antisell, M. D., of District of Columbia.
Superintendent of Propagating Garden : Wm. Saunders, of Penn.

GOVERNMENT PRINTING OFFICE.

Congressional Printer : Aaron M. Clapp, of New York.
Chief Clerk : Harry H. Clapp, of New York.

DEPARTMENT OF EDUCATION.

Commissioner of Education : General J. A. Eaton, of Tennessee.
Chief Clerk : Henry E. Rockwell, of Connecticut.

THE LEGISLATIVE BRANCH OF THE GOVERNMENT.

THE National Legislature consists of a Senate of two members from each State, making the full Senate now consist of seventy-four members, and a House of Representatives, now having two hundred and forty-five members. The Senators are chosen by the Legislatures of their several States, for a term of six years, either by concurrent vote or by joint ballot, as the State may prescribe. The members of the House of Representatives are usually elected by a plurality vote in districts of each State, whose bounds are prescribed by the Legislature, for the term of two years. In a few instances they have been elected at large : *i. e.*, by the plurality vote of the entire State.

The Constitution requires nine years' citizenship to qualify for admission to the Senate, and seven years to the House of Representatives. An act approved July 26, 1866, requires the Legislature of each State which shall be chosen next preceding the expiration of any Senatorial term, on the second Tuesday after its first meeting, to elect a successor, each House nominating *viva voce*, and then convening in Joint Assembly to compare nominations. In case of agreement, such person shall be declared duly elected; and if they do not agree, then balloting to continue from day to day at 12 M. during the session until choice has been made. Vacancies are to be filled in like manner. The members of each House receive a salary of $5,000 per annum, and mileage at the rate of twenty cents per mile. For each day's absence, except when caused by sickness, $8 per diem is deducted from the salary. The President *pro tem.* of the Senate receives the same compensation as the Vice-President. The Speaker of the House of Representatives receives double the salary of a member.

CONGRESSIONAL DISTRICTS.

The House of Representatives of the United States is composed of members elected by Districts. The number apportioned to the States has varied at each decennial census, as shown by the following Table :

Census.	When Apportioned.	Whole No. Rep.	Ratio, One to
	By Constitution	65	—
1790	April 14, 1792	105	33,000
1800	Jan. 14, 1802	141	23,000
1810	Dec. 21, 1811	151	35,000
1820	March 7, 1822	212	40,000
1830	May 22, 1832	240	46,700
1840	June 25, 1843	223	70,600
1850	July 30, 1852	233	93,423
1860	April —, 1861	242	127,000

In the new apportionment for 1870, the basis of representation will probably be about one Congressman to every 155,000 of the population.

Popular Vote for President.

Electoral Vote, 1868.	STATES.	Seymour, Dem.	Grant, Rep.	Dem. Majority	Rep. Majority	McClellan, Dem.	Lincoln, Rep.	Dem. Majority	Rep. Majority	Douglas, Dem.	Br'k'n ridge, Dem.	Bell, Union	Lincoln, Rep.
8	Alabama	72090	73501		5221					13651	48831	27875	……
5	Arkansas	19955	22133		2154					5227	28739	20094	……
5	California	54077	54593		504	43841	62134		18293	38516	34334	6817	39173
6	Connecticut	47844	50700		2934	42285	44601		2406	15522	14641	3291	43792
3	Delaware	10951	7609	3346		8767	8155	612		1023	7337	3864	3815
3	Florida	electors chosen by legislature								367	8543	5437	……
9	Georgia	101767	57130	44660						11590	51889	42886	122161
16	Illinois	199141	250293		51152	158730	189994		30764	160215	2404	4913	130033
13	Indiana	166980	176552		9572	130233	150422		20189	115509	12295	5306	70409
8	Iowa	74040	120399		46359	49591	88907		39412	55111	1048	1763	……
3	Kansas	13628	30092		16401	64301	16441		1278				1364
11	Kentucky	115884	97011	16322						25651	53143	66058	C2811
7	Louisiana	43197	7046	31914		46095	27768		21123	7625	22681	20634	2294
7	Maine	42396	30445		26098	39273	68114		7414	7035	6368	9046	106533
7	Maryland	62354	136531		74271	48717	40155		7799	5906	42482	41700	88460
12	Massachusetts	59103	113292		54189	74404	91321		16911	34372	5039	52231	22069
8	Michigan	82331	113292		30996	17337	21064		7685	63057	805	405	……
4	Minnesota	2638	24415		15386					3983	748	C8	17028
7	Mississippi	55866	83995		24092	31676	72276		41076	5890	40797	23040	……
11	Missouri	5438	9729		4451	6394	9624		3925	58372	31317	58372	17028
3	Nebraska	6217	6461		1957	32971	36400		3527				37519
3	Nevada	20571	30217		764	60024	60724		674	23681	2112	441	58324
5	N. Hampshire	8276C	419983		8895	36198C	368736	7301		65401			362646
7	New Jersey	42999	92293		41191					312510	48539	44900	231610
33	New York	84031	240922		289597	205306	265154		59596	2701	11403	12194	5570
9	N. Carolina	239931	10000	165	6645	8457	988		1431	187232	5006	183	26060
21	Ohio	1112C	342920		1767	276316	296391		2007C	3951	178871	19776	12244
3	Oregon	6349	129993		3044	6718	14346		5631	16765			
26	Pennsylva.	42357	62116		31777			electors chosen by legislature		7707		60974	
4	Rhode Isl'd	26311	56755		883	13321	42419		29099	11350	64709	60974	33408
6	S. Carolina	4406	29115		24159	10438	223152		19714	684	47548	15438	1929
6	Tennessee	1230C	108947			6384	63456		17574	16290	74323	74681	86110
5	Texas	20929								65021	889	161	
8	Vermont	84695											
	Total												
	Total Vote.	2648830	2985031	184520	390721	1811754	2230915	44498	435700	1375157	847953	590631	1866459
		5633661				4031769				4660193			

Presidents prior to the Adoption of the Constitution.

NAME.	State.	Date of Appointment.	Born.	Died.
Peyton Randolph	Virginia	September 5, 1774	1723	1775
Henry Middleton	South Carolina	October 22, 1774	……	1793
John Hancock	Massachusetts	May 24, 1775	1737	1793
Henry Laurens	South Carolina	November 1, 1777	1723	1792
John Jay	New York	December 10, 1779	1745	1829
Samuel Huntington	Connecticut	September 28, 1779	1732	1796
Thomas McKean	Delaware	July 10, 1781	1734	1817
John Hanson	Maryland	November 5, 1781	……	1783
Elias Boudinot	New Jersey	November 4, 1782	1740	1821
Thomas Mifflin	Pennsylvania	November 3, 1783	1744	1800
Richard Henry Lee	Virginia	November 30, 1784	1732	1794
Nathaniel Gorham	Massachusetts	June 6, 1786	1738	1796
Arthur St. Clair	Pennsylvania	February 2, 1787	……	1818
Cyrus Griffin	Virginia	January 22, 1788	1748	1810

Presidents under the Federal Constitution.

Names.	Inaugurated.	Born.	Age at Inauguration.	Years in office.	Died.	Age at Death.
1. George Washington, of Virginia ..	April 30, 1789	1732	57	8	Dec. 14, 1799	63
2. John Adams, of Massachusetts ...	Mar. 4—1797	1735	62	4	July 4—1826	91
3. Thomas Jefferson, of Virginia	Mar. 4—1801	1743	58	8	July 4—1826	83
4. James Madison, of Virginia	Mar. 4—1809	1751	58	8	June 28, 1836	85
5. James Monroe, of Virginia	Mar. 4—1817	1759	58	8	July 4—1831	72
6. John Quincy Adams, of Mass	Mar. 4—1825	1767	58	4	Feb. 23, 1848	80
7. Andrew Jackson, of Tennessee ..	Mar. 4—1829	1767	62	8	June 8—1845	78
8. Martin Van Buren, of New York	Mar. 4—1837	1782	55	4	July 24, 1862	79
9. William Henry Harrison, of Ohio	Mar. 4—1841	1773	68	—	April 14, 1841	68
10. John Tyler, of Virginia, Vice-President, succeeded President Harrison, who died April 4, 1841........		1790	57	4	Jan. 17, 1862	72
11. James K. Polk, of Tennessee	Mar. 4—1845	1795	49	4	June 15, 1849	54
12. Zachary Taylor, of Louisiana ...	Mar. 4—1849	1784	65	1	July 9—1850	66
13. Millard Fillmore, of N. Y., Vice-President, succeeded Pres. Taylor, who died July 9, 1850............		1800	50	3		
14. Franklin Pierce, of N. Hampshire	Mar. 4—1853	1804	49	4	Oct. 8—1869	65
15. James Buchanan, of Pennsylvania	Mar. 4—1857	1791	65	4	June 1—1869	77
16. Abraham Lincoln, of Illinois......	Mar. 4—1861	1809	52	4	April 15, 1865	56
17. Andrew Johnson, Vice-President, succeeded President Lincoln, who was assassinated April 14, 1865 ...		1803	57	4		
18. Ulysses S. Grant, of Illinois	Mar. 4—1869	1822	47	—		

Vice-Presidents.

Names.	Inaugurated.	Born.	Died.
1. John Adams, of Massachusetts	1789	1735	1826
2. Thomas Jefferson, of Virginia	1797	1743	1826
3. Aaron Burr, of New York	1801	1756	1836
4. George Clinton, of New York	1805	1739	1819
5. Elbridge Gerry, of Massachusetts..............	1813	1744	1814
6. Daniel D. Tompkins, of New York	1817	1744	1825
7. John C. Calhoun, of South Carolina ..:.........	1825	1782	1850
8. Martin Van Buren, of New York ......'.......	1833	1782	1862
9. Richard M. Johnson, of Kentucky	1837	1780	1850
10. John Tyler, of Virginia	1841	1790	1862
11. George M. Dallas, of Pennsylvania	1845	1792	1863
12. Millard Fillmore, of New York	1849	1800	
13. William R. King, of Alabama.................	1853	1786	1853
14. John C. Breckenridge, of Kentucky	1857	1821	
15. Hannibal Hamlin, of Maine...................	1861	1809	
16. Andrew Johnson, of Tennessee	1865	1808	
17. Schuyler Colfax, of Indiana	1869	1823	

NOTE.—The Vice-President acts as President of the Senate.

Chief Justices of the Supreme Court of the United States.

Name.	State.	Term of Service.	Born.	Died.
John Jay	New York	1789—1795	1745	1829
John Rutledge	South Carolina..	1795—1795	1739	1800
Oliver Ellsworth.....................	Connecticut......	1796—1801	1752	1807
John Marshall.......................	Virginia	1801—1836	1755	1835
Roger B. Taney......................	Maryland	1836—1864	1777	1864
Salmon P. Chase.....................	Ohio	1864— ...	1808	....

Associate Justices of the Supreme Court of the United States.

NAME.	State.	Term of Service.	Born.	Died.
John Rutledge	South Carolina...	1789—1791	1739	1800
William Cushing.....................	Massachusetts....	1789—1810	1733	1810
James Wilson........................	Pennsylvania	1789—1798	1742	1798
John Blair...........................	Virginia	1789—1796	1732	1800
Robert H. Harrison..................	Maryland	1789—1789	1745	1790
James Iredell........................	North Carolina...	1790—1799	1750	1799
Thomas Johnson.....................	Maryland	1791—1793	1772	1819
William Patterson...................	New Jersey.......	1793—1806	1745	1806

Associate Justices of the Supreme Court of the U. S. (Continued.)

Name.	State.	Term of Service.	Born.	Died.
Samuel Chase	Maryland	1796—1811	1741	1811
Bushrod Washington	Virginia	1798—1829	1759	1829
Alfred Moore	North Carolina	1799—1804	1755	1810
William Johnston	South Carolina	1804—1834	1771	1834
Brockholst Livingston	New York	1806—1823	1757	1823
Thomas Todd	Kentucky	1807—1826	1765	1826
Joseph Story	Massachusetts	1811—1845	1779	1845
Gabriel Duval	Maryland	1811—1835	1751	1844
Smith Thompson	New York	1823—1845	1767	1845
Robert Trimble	Kentucky	1826—1829	1776	1829
John McLean	Ohio	1829—1861	1785	1861
Henry Baldwin	Pennsylvania	1830—1846	1779	1846
James M. Wayne	Georgia	1835—1867	1786	1867
Philip H. Barbour	Virginia	1836—1841	1779	1841
John Catron	Tennessee	1837—1865	1786	1865
John McKinley	Alabama	1837—1852	....	1852
Peter V. Daniel	Virginia	1841—1860	1785	1860
Samuel Nelson	New York	1845—	1792	....
Levi Woodbury	New Hampshire	1845—1851	1790	1851
Robert C. Grier	Pennsylvania	1846—1870	1794	1870
Benjamin R. Curtis	Massachusetts	1851—1857	1809	....
James A. Campbell	Alabama	1853—1856	1802	....
Nathan Clifford	Maine	1858—	1803	....
Noah H. Swayne	Ohio	1862—	1805	....
Samuel F. Miller	Iowa	1862—	1816	....
David Davis	Illinois	1862—	1815	....
Stephen J. Field	California	1863—	1817	....
William Strong	Pennsylvania	1870—	....	....
Joseph P. Bradley	New Jersey	1870	....	....

APPORTIONMENT OF REPRESENTATIVES.

By Act of 1872, *under the census of* 1870.

Alabama 7	Kansas 3	Nebraska 1	Rhode Island 2
Arkansas 4	Kentucky 10	Nevada 1	South Carolina ... 5
California 4	Louisiana 5	New Hampshire .. 2	Tennessee 9
Connecticut 4	Maine 5	New Jersey 7	Texas 6
Delaware......... 1	Maryland 6	New York 32	Virginia 9
Florida 1	Massachusetts ...11	North Carolina.... 8	Vermont 2
Georgia 9	Michigan 9	Ohio..............20	West Virginia ... 3
Illinois 19	Minnesota 3	Oregon 1	Wisconsin 8
Indiana 12	Mississippi........ 6	Pennsylvania.....26	
Iowa 9	Missouri.........13		Total 283

The ratio of apportionment is about 142,000 inhabitants for a Member of Congress, though allowance is made for fractions in excess of one-half.

PUBLIC DEBT OF THE UNITED STATES
March 1, 1872.

Debt bearing Interest in Coin.

Bonds at 6 per cent	$1,467,750,500 00
Bonds at 5 per cent	382,399,700 00
Principal	$1,850,150,200 00
Interest	32,899,227 89

Debt bearing Interest in Lawful Money.

Certificates of Indebtedness at 4 per cent	$678,000 00
Navy Pension Fund at 3 per cent	14,000.000 00
Certificates at 3 per cent	19.140,000 00
Principal	$33,818,000 00
Interest	248,418 82

Debt on which Interest has ceased since maturity.

Principal	$1,679,142 26
Interest	270,208 54

Debt bearing no Interest.

Old Demand and Legal-Tender Notes	$357,591,101 25
Fractional Currency	41,491,300 43
Coin Certificates	32,520,000 00
Principal	$431,602,401 68
Unclaimed Interest	14,644 05

Total Debt.

Principal	$2,317,249,743 94
Interest	33,432,299 69
Total	$2,350,682,243 83

Cash in the Treasury.

Coin	$110,405,319 02
Currency	14,463,426 83
Total	$124,868,745 85
Debt, less cash in the Treasury, March 1, 1872	2,225,813,497 98
Debt, less cash in the Treasury, February 1, 1872	2,238,204,949 50
Decrease of debt during the past month	12,391,451 52
Decrease of debt since March 1, 1871	94,895.348 94
Decrease of debt from March 1, 1869, to March 1, 1872	290,649,762 03

Bonds issued to Pacific Railway Companies, Interest payable in Lawful Money.

Principal outstanding	$64,623,512 00
Interest accrued and not yet paid	646,235 00
Interest paid by the United States	14,631,870 00
Interest repaid by transportation of mails, etc	3,477,125 00
Balance of interest paid by the United States	11,154,745 00

Statement of Bonds purchased by the Treasury Department, which have been cancelled and destroyed.

Principal of the bonds	$217,192,350 00
Amount paid in currency	244,029,656 00
Currency value of accrued Interest on bonds bought flat	3,084.892 00
Net cash in currency	243,998.807 97
Net cost estimated in gold	202,490,985 00

REDUCTION OF THE NATIONAL DEBT OF THE UNITED STATES
for three years—March 1869 *to March* 1872.

	Debt of the United States less cash in the Treasury.	Decrease of debt during the preceding month.	Total decrease since Mar. 1, 1869, to date.	Monthly interest charge.	Decrease in monthly interest charge.	Decrease in annual interest charge.
1869.						
Mar. 1	2,525,463,260 01	....	....	10,532,462 50	....	....
April 1	2,525,196,461 74	266,798 27	....	10,526,238 00	6,224 50	74,694 00
May 1	2,518,797,391 09	6,399,070 65	6,665,868 92	10,522,835 75	9,625 75	115,521 00
June 1	2,505,412,613 12	13,384,777 97	20,050,646 89	10,507,090 25	25,372 25	304,467 00
July 1	2,489,002,480 58	16,410,132 54	36,460,779 43	10,476,840 25	55,622 25	667,467 00
Aug. 1	2,481,566,736 29	7,435,744 29	43,896,523 72	10,383,568 75	148,893 75	1,786,725 00
Sept. 1	2,475,962,501 50	5,604,234 79	49,500,758 51	10,333,518 75	198,943 75	2,387,325 00
Oct. 1	2,468,495,072 11	7,467,429 39	56,968,187 90	10,252,933 75	279,528 75	3,354,345 00
Nov. 1	2,461,131,189 36	7,363,882 75	64,332,070 65	10,194,903 75	337,558 75	4,050,705 00
Dec. 1	2,453,559,735 23	7,571,454 13	71,903,524 78	10,130,625 75	401,836 75	4,822,041 00
1870.						
Jan. 1	2,448,746,953 31	4,812,781 92	76,716,306 70	10,061,506 25	470,956 25	5,651,475 00
Feb. 1	2,444,813,289 92	3,933,664 39	80,649,971 09	10,022,498 00	509,964 50	6,119,574 00
Mar. 1	2,438,328,477 17	6,484,811 75	87,134,782 84	10,007,312 75	525,149 75	6,301,797 00
April 1	2,432,562,127 74	5,762,349 43	92,901,132 27	9,982,350 00	550,112 50	6,601,350 00
May 1	2,420,864,334 35	11,697,793 39	104,598,925 66	9,956,759 50	575 703 00	6,908,436 00
June 1	2,405,562,371 78	14,301,962 57	118,990,888 23	9,926,762 75	605,699 75	7,268,397 00
July 1	2,346,358,599 74	20,203,772 04	139,104,660 27	9,896,812 75	645,649 75	7,747,797 00
Aug. 1	2,339,324,476 00	17,034,123 74	156,138,784 01	9,854,633 00	677,829 50	8,133,954 00
Sept. 1	2,315,921,150 41	13,403,325 59	169,542,109 60	9,814,590 00	717,872 50	8,614,470 00
Oct. 1	2,346,913,652 29	9,007,498 13	178,549,607 73	9,768,940 00	763,522 50	9,162,270 00
Nov. 1	2,341,784,355 55	5,129,296 73	183,678,904 46	9,718,436 52	814,025 92	9,768,311 04
Dec. 1	2,334,308,494 05	7,475,860 90	191,154,765 36	9,686,164 42	846,298 08	10,155,576 96
1871.						
Jan. 1	2,332,067,793 75	2,240,700 90	193,395,466 26	9,644,043 63	898,418 87	10,661,026 44
Feb. 1	2,328,026,897 00	4,040,986 75	197,436,453 01	9,610,386 13	922,076 37	11,064,916 44
Mar. 1	2,320,709,846 92	7,317,960 08	204,754,413 09	9,571,007 41	961,455 09	11,537,461 08
April 1	2,309,697,596 27	11,011,250 65	215,765,663 74	9,527,212 67	1,005,249 83	12,062,997 96
May 1	2,303,573,543 14	6,124,053 13	221,889,716 87	9,459,959 17	1,072,503 33	12,870,039 96
June 1	2,299,134,184 81	4,439,358 33	226,329,075 20	9,408,362 33	1,124,100 17	13,489,202 04
July 1	2,292,030,834 90	7,103,349 91	233,432,425 11	9,329,110 87	1,203,351 63	14,440,219 56
Aug. 1	2,283,328,857 98	8,701,976 92	242,134,402 03	9,382,345 50	1,230,117 00	14,761,404 00
Sept. 1	2,274,122,560 38	9,206,297 60	251,340,699 63	9,296,615 46	1,945,847 04	14,950,164 48
Oct. 1	2,260,663,939 87	13,458,620 51	264,799,320 14	9,248,001 83	1,284,460 67	15,413,524 04
Nov. 1	2,251,713,443 03	8,950,491 84	273,749,811 98	9,168,453 42	1,364,009 08	16,368,108 96
Dec. 1	2,248,251,367 85	3,462,080 18	277,211,892 16	9,137,342 83	1,395,119 67	16,741,436 04
1872.						
Jan. 1	2,243,838,411 14	4,412,956 71	281,624,848 87	9,101,968 54	1,430,493 96	17,165,927 52
Feb. 1	2,238,204,949 50	5,633,461 64	287,258,310 51	9,065,892 96	1,466,569 54	17,598,834 48
Mar. 1	2,225,813,497 98	12,391,451 52	299,649,762 03	....	....	....

DEBT OF EACH ADMINISTRATION.

The Public Debt at the close of each administration, since the adoption of the constitution was:

Washington's first term.............	1793	$80,352,630
do second term.........	1797	82,064,479
John Adams..................	1801	82,038,050
Jefferson's first term..........	1805	82,312,150
do second term...........	1809	57,023,192
Madison's first term..............	1813	59,962,827
do second term............	1817	123,491,965
Monroe's first term...............	1821	89,987,427
do second term............	1825	83,788,432
John Quincy Adams...............	1829	59,421,413
Jackson's first term	1833	7,001,022
In	1836	291,089
do second term...........	1837	1,875,312
Van Buren......................	1841	6,488,784
Tyler.......................	1845	17,093,794
Polk	1849	64,704,693
Fillmore	1853	67,340,620
Pierce	1857	29,060,387
Buchanan..........................	1861	90,867,828
Lincoln..........................	1865	2,682,593,026
Johnson.................January 1,	1866	2,810,310,357
Johnson.................March 4,	1869	2,491,399,904
Grant.................April 1,	1871	2,268,316,231

UNITED STATES LOANS.

Subjoined will be found a list of the recent United States loans, with the amount of the same, date of creation, etc. For the present condition of such of these loans, as possess vital contemporaneous interest, the reader is referred to the statement of the Public Debt in this volume:

Fives of 1874.—Dated January 1, 1859; payable after January 1, 1874. Interest, 5 per cent., in coin; payable 1st of January and July. Registered bonds, $5,000; coupon bonds, $1,000. Amount authorized and issued, $20,000,000. [Act June 14, 1858.]

Fives of 1871.—Dated January 1, 1861; payable after January 1. 1871, and before January 1, 1881. Interest, 5 per cent.. in coin; payable 1st of January and July. Registered bonds, $1,000 and $5,000; coupon bonds, $1,000. Amount authorized, $21,0000,000; issued $7,022,000. [Act June 22, 1860.]

Oregon War Loan.—Dated July 1, 1861; payable July 1, 1881. Interest 6 per cent., in coin; payable 1st of January and July. The bonds are made payable to order, with coupons attached, payable to bearer. Denominations $50, $100 and $500. Amount authorized, $2,800,-000; issued $1,090,850. [Act March 2, 1861.]

Sixes of 1881.—(First issue.) Dated 1861 ; payable after December 31, 1880. Interest 6 per cent., in coin; payable 1st of January and July. Registered bonds, $1,000, $5,000 and $10,000; coupon bonds $1,000. Amount authorized $25,000,000; issued $18,415,000. [Act February 8, 1861.]

Sixes of 1881.—(Second issue.) Dated November 16, 1861; payable after June 30, 1881. Interest 6 per cent. in coin; payable 1st of January and July. Registered bonds, $50, $100, $500, $1,000, $5,000 and $10,000 ;·coupon bonds $50, $100, $500 and $1,000. Amount authorized, $189,999,750· issued 189,317,400. 'Acts July 17 and August 5, 1861.]

The act of July 17 authorized the issue of $50,000,000 in 1881s and $139,999,750 and 7 3–10s. The act of August 5, 1861, authorized the conversion of 7 3–10s into 1881s.

Sixes of 1881.—(Third issue.) Dated June 15, 1864; payable after June 30, 1881. Interest 6 per cent.; payable 1st of January and July; principal and interest payable in coin. Registered bonds, $50, $100, $500, $1,000, $5,000, and $10,000 ; coupon bonds, $50, $100, $500 and $1,000. Amount authorized and issued, $75,000,000. [Act March 3, 1863.]

UNITED STATES LOANS—(Continued.)

This is the first loan act which specifically provides for payment *in coin* of *principal* (as well as interest) of the bonds issued under its authority.

Five-Twenties of 1862.—Dated May 1, 1862 ; redeemable after May 1, 1867, and payable May 1, 1882. Interest 6 per cent. in coin ; payable 1st of May and November. Registered bonds, $50, $100, $500, $1,000, $5,000 and $10,000 ; coupon bonds, $50, $100, $500 and $1,000. Amount authorized, act February 25, 1862, $500,000,000 ; amount authorized, supplementary act March 3, 1864, $11,000,000 ; amount authorized supplementary act January 28, 1865, $4,000,000 ; amount issued, $514,771,-600. [Act February 25, 1862, and supplementary acts.]

Five-Twenties of 1864.—Dated November 1, 1864 ; redeemable after November 1, 1869, and payable November 1, 1884. Interest, 6 per cent., in coin ; payable 1st of May and November. Registered bonds, $50, $100, $500, $1,000, $5,000 and $10,000 ; coupon bonds $50, $100, $500 and $1,000. Issued under act March 3, 1864, $3,882,500 ; issued under act June 30, 1864, $125,561,300. Total issue, 129,443,800. [Act March 3, 1864, and June 30, 1864.]

Those bonds issued under the act of March 3, 1864, are, by the provisions of that act, payable *in coin*, and are issued in registered bonds only ; but the amount being comparatively small, no distinction is made between them and the other issue.

Five-Twenties of 1865.—Dated November 1, 1865 ; redeemable after November 1, 1870, and payable November 1, 1885 ; interest, 6 per cent., in coin ; payable on the 1st of May and November. Registered bonds, $50, $100, $500, $1,000, $5,000, and $10,000 ; coupon bonds, $50, $100, $500 and $1,000. Amount issued, $203,327,250. [Act March 3, 1865.]

Five-Twenties of 1865.—(January and July issue.) Dated July 1, 1865 ; redeemable after July 1, 1870, and payable July 1, 1885. Interest 6 per cent. in coin ; payable 1st of January and July. Registered bonds, $50, $100, $500, $1,000, $5,000 and $10,000 ; coupon bonds, 50, $100, $500 and $1,000. Amount issued, $332,998,950. [Act March 3, 1865.]

Five-Twenties of 1867.—Dated July 1, 1867 ; redeemable after July 1, 1872, and payable July 1, 1887. Interest 6 per cent., in coin ; payable 1st of January and July. Registered bonds, $50, $100, 500, $1,000, $5,000 and $10,000 ; coupon bonds $50, $100, $500 and $1,000. Amount issued, $379,506,400. [Act March 3, 1865.]

Five-Twenties of 1868.—Dated July 1, 1868 ; redeemable after July 1, 1873, and payable July 1, 1888. Interest 6 per cent. in coin. ; payable 1st of January and July. Registered bonds $50, $100, $500, $1,000, $5,000 and $10,000 ; coupon bonds, $50, $100, $500 and $1,000. Amount issued $42,539,350. [Act March 3, 1865.]

UNITED STATES LOANS—(Continued.)

Ten-Forties.—Dated March 1, 1864; redeemable after March 1, 1874, and payable March 1, 1904. Interest 5 per cent.; payable 1st of March and September, excepting coupon bonds of $50 and $100, the interest on which is payable annually on 1st of March. Principal and interest payable in coin. Registered bonds, $50, $100, $500, $1,000, $5,000 and $10,000; coupon bonds, $50, $100, $500 and $1,000. Amount authorized, $200,000,000. Issued, $194,567,300. [Act March 3, 1864.]

This act, like that of March 3, 1863, provides for payment *in coin of principal* (as well as interest) of bonds issued under its authority.

United States Currency Sixes.—(Pacific R. R. bonds.) Dated Jan. 16, 1865, and variously thereafter, and payable 30 years from date. Interest 6 per cent., in lawful money; payable 1st of January and 1st of July. Registered bonds, $1,000, $5,000 and $10,000; no coupon bonds issued. Amount issued to September 1, 1870, $64,618,832. [Acts July 1, 1862, and July 2, 1864.]

Fives of 1870.—Redeemable at the pleasure of the United States, after May 1, 1881, in gold. Interest, five per cent. in gold, payable quarterly—February, May, August and November 1st. Exempt from all taxation. Issued under Acts of July 14, 1870, and Jan. 20, 1871. Amount, $200,000,000. All disposed of; about $120,000,000 being sold in Europe. The proceeds of these bonds are used in redeeming the Five-Twenties. A still larger amount of five per cents., four and a half per cents. and four per cents. are authorized for the same purpose, and will probably be placed in 1872 and 1873.

Gold Certificates.—Payable to bearer on demand, and bearing no interest. Denominations, $20, $50, $100, $500, 1,000 and $5,000. [Act March 3, 1863.]

The amount of these certificates outstanding is increased and diminished to meet the public demand, but cannot be more than 20 per cent. in excess of the amount of coin and bullion in the Treasury. Amount, March 1, 1869, $20,775,560.

IMMIGRATION.

IMMIGRATION FROM 1820 to 1871.

By an Act of Congress, approved March 2, 1819, Collectors of Customs were required to keep a record, and make a quarterly return to the Treasury of all passengers arriving in their respective districts from Foreign Ports ; and these reports, duly condensed in the Department, are the chief bases of our knowledge of the subsequent growth and progress of Immigration. Total number of foreign-born passengers arriving at the ports of the United States in the several years from 1820 to 1871, inclusive, are as follows :

1820 8,385	1833 58,640	1846 154,416	1859 121,282
1821 9,127	1834 65,365	1847 234,968	1860 153,640
1822 6,911	1835 45,374	1848 226,527	1861 91,920
1823 6,354	1836 76,242	1849 297,024	1862 91,987
1824 7,912	1837 79,340	1850 369,980	1863 176,282
1825 10,199	1838 39,914	1851 379,466	1864 193,418
1826 10,837	1839 68,069	1852 371,603	1865 248,120
1827 18,875	1840 84,066	1853 368,645	1866 318,554
1828 27,382	1841 80,289	1854 427,833	1867 298,358
1829 22,520	1842 104,565	1855 200,877	1868 297,215
1830 23,322	1843 52,496	1856 200,436	1869 389,051
1831 22,633	1844 78,615	1857 251,306	1870 387,098
1832 60,482	1845 114,371	1858 123,126	1871 321,350

Of the Immigrants who landed on our shores in the *forty years* ending with 1860 (1820 to 1860) there came from different countries as follows :

Great Britain and Ireland 2,750,874	S. America... 6,201	Germany ...1,546,476	Portugal.... 2,014
France 208,063	The Azores .. 3,242	Holland..... 21,579	Poland...... 1,659
West Indies. 40,487	Sardinia...... 2,030	Mexico 17,706	All other and not stated.. 218,140
Sweden and Norway... 36,120	Russia 1,374	Italy........ 11,202	
	Switzerland .. 37,733	Belgium..... 9,862	Total 5,062,414
	China 41,443	Denmark ... 5,543	

Total from 1860 to 1870 2,492,601
Estimated from 1763 to 1820 300,000

Grand Total (exclusive of African birth and Immigrants from Canada)...........7,855,015

Of those arriving here from January 1st, 1820, to September 30th, 1870, those wholly or mainly speaking English were from

England............. 501,316	British America...... 271,185	New Zealand 17
Ireland............. 1,406,030	Australia............ 243	Sandwich Islands 35
Scotland............. 82,403	Azores.............. 6,636	Malta................. 127
Wales............... 12,213	Bermudas........... 61	Jamaica............. 83
Great Britain (not specified) 1,824,073	St. Helena........... 33	
	Cape of Good Hope .. 88	Of English speech..4,104,553

Of races mainly Teutonic or Scandinavian there were from

Germany	2,250,922	Belgium	16,850	Iceland	11
Prussia	100,963	Switzerland	61,209	Total Germanic and	
Austria	7,994	Denmark	23,221	Scandinavian	2,643,069
Holland	30,905	Sweden and Norway	151,104		

Of Slavic races, Russians, Poles and Hungarians 7,373

Of French, Spanish, Portuguese and Italian races there were from

France	245,147	Central America	1,067	Cape Verd, Madeira,	
Spain	23,096	S. American States	7,692	and Canaries	674
Portugal	4,416	Cuba	3,960	Miquelon	3
Italy	23,397	Hayti	81	Corsica	11
Sardinia	2,103	Porto Rico	50	Sicily	675
Mexico	29,039	Other West Indies	43,458	Total French,	
				Spanish, etc.	377,889

Of Asiatic and Polynesian races there were from

China	108,600	Total Asiatic, etc.	109,169	Countries not	
The rest of Asia and		*African Nations*	571	specified	205,807
Asiatic Islands	547	*Turkey*	299		
Polynesia	12	*Greece*	195	Aggregate 1820–1870	7,448,925

Of the 2,340,928 passengers landed at Castle Garden from August 1st, 1855, to January 1st, 1870, their avowed destinations were as follows:

						Other Countries.	
New York and		South Carolina	1,854	Missouri	44,309		
undecided	972,267	Georgia	1,623	Minnesota	29,360	Canada	50,828
Maine	4,013	Florida	190	Kansas	5,652	New Brunswick	1,028
New Hamps.	2,859	Alabama	577	Nebraska	4,198	New Dominion	816
Vermont	4,405	Mississippi	603	Dakota	49	South America	506
Massachusetts	111,129	Louisiana	4,353	Colorado	170	Cuba	349
Rhode Island	21,430	Texas	1,522	Wyoming	5	Mexico	220
Connecticut	39,169	Arkansas	302	Utah	23,735	Bermudas and	
New Jersey	63,109	Tennessee	4,171	Montana	33	other W. In.	143
Pennsylvania	224,890	Kentucky	11,657	Idaho	32	Central Am.	113
Delaware	2,011	Ohio	120,448	Nevada	80	N. W. Coast	473
Maryland	19,033	Michigan	52,205	New Mexico	50	Australia	13
Dist. Columbia	9,129	Indiana	29,576	California	22,823	Sandwich Is.	1
Virginia	8235	Illinois	213,315	Oregon and		Japan	1
West Virginia	172	Wisconsin	121,660	Wash. Terri.	195	China	6
North Carolina	784	Iowa	44,286			Unknown	22,035

INTERNAL REVENUE.

THESE rates are those of the new Internal Revenue Law, passed June, 1872, and taking effect October 1, 1872.

TAXES.

Ale, per bbl. of 31 gallons $1 00
Banks, on average amount of deposits, each month ....1-24 of 1 ₱ ct.
Bank deposits, savings, etc., having no capital stock, per six months ¼ of 1 ₱ ct.
Banks, on capital, beyond the average amount invested in United States bonds, each month...1-24 of 1 ₱ ct.
Banks, on average amount of circulation, each month ....1-12 of 1 ₱ ct.
Banks, on average amount of circulation, beyond 90 per cent. of the capital, an additional tax each month .... 1-6 of 1 ₱ ct.
Banks, on amount of notes of any person, state bank, or state banking association, used and paid out as circulation ....10 ₱ ct.
Beer, per bbl. of 31 gallons... $1 00
Brandy, made from grapes, per gallon 70
Brewers, special tax on 100 00
Chewing tobacco, fine cut, plug, or twist, per lb....................... 20
Cigars, manufacturers of, special tax................................... 10 00
Cigars, of all descriptions, made of tobacco or any substitute therefor, per 100 .... 5 00
Cigars, imported, in addition to import duty to pay same as above.
Cigarettes, not weighing more than 3 lbs. per 1,000, per 1,000 .... 1 50
Cigarettes, weight exceeding 3 lbs. per 1,000, per 1,000................. 5 00
Dealers in leaf tobacco, wholesale...................................... 25 00
Dealers in leaf tobacco, retail.. 5 00
Dealers in leaf tobacco, for sales in excess of $1,000, per dollar of excess 5
Distilled spirits, every proof gallon 70
Distillers, producing 100 bbls. or less (40 gallons of proof spirit to bbl) per annum.. 400 00
Distillers, for each bbl. in excess of 100 bbls........................ 4 00
Distillers, on each bbl. of 40 gallons in warehouse when act took effect, and when withdrawn 4 00
Distillers of brandy from grapes, peaches, and apples exclusively, producing less than 150 bbls. annually, special tax $50, and $4 per bbl. of 40 gallons.
Distillery, having aggregate capacity for mashing, etc., 20 bushels of grain per day, or less per day.. 2 00
Distillery, in excess of 20 bushels of grain per day, for every 20 bushels, per day.. 2 00
Fermented liquors, in general, per bbl 1 00

Gas, coal, illuminating, when the product shall not be above 200,000 cubic feet per month, per 1,000 cubic feet 10

Gas, coal, when product exceeds 200,000, and does not exceed 500,000 cubic feet per month, per 1,000 cubic feet 15

Gas, coal, when product exceeds 500,000, and does not exceed 5,000,000 cubic feet per month, per 1,000 cubic feet ....,......... 20

Gas, coal, when product exceeds 5,000,000 feet per month, per 1,000 cubic feet 25

Imitation wines and champagne, not made from grapes, currants, rhubarb, or berries, grown in the United States, rectified or mixed, to be sold as wine or any other name, per dozen bottles of more than a pint and not more than a quart.................................... 2 40

Imitation wines, containing not more than one pint, per dozen bottles.. 1 20

Lager beer, per bbl. of 31 gallons 1 00

Liquors, dealers in, whose sales, including sales of all other merchandise, shall exceed $25,000, an additional tax for every $100 on sales of liquors in excess of such $25,000..................................... 1 00

Manufacturers of stills 50 00

Manufacturers of stills, for each still or worm made.................,...... 20 00

Porter, per bbl. of 31 gallons 1 00

Rectifiers, special tax 200 00

Retail liquor dealers, special tax....................................... 25 00

Retail malt liquor dealers 20 00

Snuff, manufactured of tobacco, or any substitute, when prepared for use, per lb... 32

Snuff-flour, sold or removed, for use, per lb............................. 32

Stamps, distillers', other than tax-paid stamps charged to collector, each 10

Tobacco, dealers in 10 00

Tobacco, manufacturers of.. 10 00

Tobacco, twisted by hand, or reduced from leaf, to be consumed, without the use of machine or instrument, and not pressed or sweetened, per lb. 20

Tobacco, all other kinds not provided for, per lb 20

Tobacco peddlers, traveling with more than two horses, mules, or other animals (first class) 50 00

Tobacco peddlers, traveling with two horses, mules, or other animals (second class) 25 00

Tobacco peddlers, traveling with one horse, mule, or other animal (third class) 15 00

Tobacco peddlers, traveling on foot, or by public conveyance (fourth class) 10 00

Tobacco, snuff and cigars, for immediate export, stamps for, each........ 10

Wholesale liquor dealers 100 00

Wholesale malt liquor dealers... 50 00

Wholesale dealers in liquors whose sales, including sales of all other merchandise, shall exceed $25,000, each to pay an additional tax on every $100 of sales of liquors in excess of $25,000 .... 1 00

STAMP DUTIES.

THE latest Internal Revenue Act of the United States (that of June, 1872), provides for the following stamp duties after October 1, 1872. All other stamp duties in Schedule B are repealed.

SCHEDULE B.

Bank check, draft, or order for the payment of any sum of money whatsoever, drawn upon any bank, banker, or trust company, or for any sum exceeding $10, drawn upon any other person or persons, companies, or corporations, at sight or on demand....................... 2

Medicines or Preparations.

SCHEDULE C.

For and upon every packet, box, bottle, pot, vial, or other inclosure, containing any pills, powders, tinctures, troches, or lozenges, syrups, cordials, bitters, anodynes, tonics, plasters, liniments, salves, ointments, pastes, drops, waters, essences, spirits, oils, or other preparations or compositions whatsoever, made and sold, or removed for consumption and sale, by any person or persons whatever, wherein the person making or preparing the same has, or claims to have, any private formula or occult secret or art for the making or preparing the same, or has, or claims to have, any exclusive right or title to the making or preparing the same, or which are prepared, uttered, vended, or exposed for sale under any letters patent, or held out or recommended to the public by the makers, venders, or proprietors thereof as proprietary medicines, or as remedies or specifics for any disease, diseases, or affections whatever affecting the human or animal body, as follows: where such packet, box, bottle, vial, or other inclosure, with its contents, shall not exceed, at the retail price or value, the sum of twenty-five cents, one cent 1
Where such packet, box, bottle, pot, vial, or other inclosure, with its contents, shall exceed the retail price or value of 25 cents, and not exceed the retail price or value of 50 cents, two cents...................... 2
Where such packet, box, bottle, pot, vial, or other inclosure, with its contents shall exceed the retail price or value of 50 cents, and shall not exceed the retail price or value of 75 cents, three cents............... 3
Where such packet, box, bottle, pot, vial, or other inclosure, with its contents, shall exceed the retail price or value of 75 cents, and shall not exceed the retail price or value of $1, four cents...................... 4
Where such packet, box, bottle, pot, vial, or other inclosure, with its contents, shall exceed the retail price or value of $1, for each and every 50 cents or fractional part thereof over and above the $1, as beforementioned, an additional two cents 2

Perfumery and Cosmetics.

For and upon every packet, box, bottle, pot, vial, or other inclosure, containing any essence, extract, toilet water, cosmetic, hair oil, pomade, hair dressing, hair restorative, hair dye, tooth wash, dentifrice, tooth paste, aromatic cachous, or any similar articles, by whatsoever name the same have been, now are, or may hereafter be called, known, or distinguished, used or applied, or to be used or applied as perfumes or applications to the hair, mouth, or skin, made, prepared, and sold or removed for consumption and sale in the United States, where such packet, box, bottle, pot, vial, or other inclosure, with its contents, shall not exceed, at the retail price or value, the sum of 25 cents, one cent..

Where such packet, bottle, box, pot, vial, or other inclosure, with its contents, shall exceed the retail price or value of 25 cents, and shall not exceed the retail price or value of 50 cents, two cents.............

Where such packet, box, bottle, pot, vial, or other inclosure, with its contents, shall exceed the retail price or value of 50 cents, and shall not exceed the retail price or value of 75 cents, three cents............

Where such packet, box, bottle, pot, vial, or other inclosure, with its contents, shall exceed the retail price or value of 75 cents, and shall not exceed the retail price or value of $1, four cents......................

Where such packet, box, bottle, pot, vial, or other inclosure, with its contents, shall exceed the retail price or value of $1, for each and every 50 cents or fractional part thereof over and above the $1, as before mentioned, an additional two cents ....

Friction matches, or lucifer matches, or other articles made in part of wood, and used for like purposes, in parcels or packages containing 100 matches or less, for each parcel or package, one cent.............

When in parcels or packages containing more than 100 and not more than 200 matches, for each parcel or package, two cents ....

And for every additional 100 matches, or fractional parts thereof, one cent..

For wax tapers, double the rates herein imposed upon friction or lucifer matches; on cigar lights, made in part of wood, wax, glass, paper, or other materials, in parcels or packages containing 25 lights or less in each parcel or package, one cent...

When in parcels or packages containing more than 25 and not more than 50 lights, two cents...

For every additional 25 lights or fractional part of that number, one cent additional...

TARIFF OF THE UNITED STATES.

THE XLIst Congress passed a Tariff Act on the 13th of July, 1870, to define the duties to be levied on raw material, manufactured goods, natural products, works of art and science, and wares of all kinds that enter the United States from foreign countries. This act went into operation January 1, 1871, but was farther materially modified in June, 1872, the changes taking effect August 1, 1872. A complete record of the goods now subject to custom-house duty, and of the goods exempt from Tariff taxation, under the amended Tariff, will be found below. The names of all goods, whether free or taxed, are arranged in alphabetical order:

ARTICLE.	TAX.
Absinthe, per proof gallon	$2 00
Acid, arsenious, crude	Free
nitric, not chemically pure	Free
muriatic, and sulphuric, except fuming (Nordhausen)	Free
oxalic, and boracic	Free
picric, and nitro-picric	Free
Aconite, root, leaf and bark	Free
oil or tincture	No tax provided
Agaric	Free
Agates, unmanufactured	Free
Albata, manufactures or articles of	45 p. c.
Albumen	Free
Ale, per proof gallon	2 00
Alkanet root	Free
Alkekengi	Free
Aluminium and its alloys, manufactures of	Free
Alloy of nickel with copper, per lb	20
Aloes	Free
Amber, gum, and beads	Free
manufactured	20 p. c.
Ammonia, crude	Free
manufactured	20 p. c.
Aniline dyes and colors, by whatever name known, 50 cts. per lb. and 35 per ct.	
Animals, live, except those brought here temporarily for exhibition	20 p. c.
Animal oil, all, per gallon	20 p. c.
Annatto seed	Free
manufactured	Free
Argentine, manufactures or articles of	45 p. c.
Argols, crude	Free

Arrack, per proof gallon 2 00
Arseniate of aniline .... Free
Arsenic .... Free
Articles imported for use of the United States, provided the price thereof
    did not include the duty .... Free
Articles produced within the United States, if exported and reimported
    in the same condition, or empty, if notice is given .... Free
Asbestos, not manufactured .... Free
          manufactured .... 25 p. c.
Balsams, copaiva, fir, Canada, Peru, Tolu, and balm of Gilead .... Free
Bamboos, unmanufactured, including those cut into lengths for canes, etc., Free
       manufactured .... 10 p. c.
Bananas .... 10 p. c.
Bark, Peruvian .... Free
     Lima .... Free
     calisaya .... Free
     canella alba .... Free
     cinchona .... Free
     croton, pomegranate, cascarilla .... Free
Barks, seeds and roots, for medicinal purposes, in a crude state .... Free
Bed feathers and downs .... Free
Bay rum, first proof, per gallon 1 00
     essence or oil, per ounce 50
Belladona, root and leaf .... Free
Bells, broken, and bell metal broken .... Free
Berries, pimento and black, white, and red or cayenne pepper, per lb... 5
Berries, including nuts and vegetables for use in manufacturing dyes,
    excepting such as enter into the composition of aniline colors .... Free
Berries, such as are or may be used in manufacturing aniline dyes, per lb. 50
The same ad valorem (in addition to tax), per lb .... 35 p. c.
Bezoar stones .... Free
Birds, stuffed .... Free
Bitters, cordials, etc., per proof gallon 2 00
Bitter apples, colocynth, coloquintida .... Free
Black salts, and black tan .... Free
Bologna sausages .... Free
Bones, unmanufactured .... Free
     ground and calcined .... Free
     dust and ashes .... Free
Books, more than twenty years old, or for libraries, or for use by their
    owners .... Free
Books, of recent date .... 22½ p. c.
Brandy, per proof gallon 2 00
Brazil pebbles, and Brazil paste .... Free
Brimstone, crude .... Free
        manufactured ....
Buchu leaves .... Free
Building stone, except marble, per ton 1 50
Burr stone in blocks, unmanufactured .... Free
     in mill stones, or manufactured .... Free
Buttons, made wholly or chiefly of silk, provided they contain no wool,
    worsted, or goat's hair, ad valorem .... 50 p. c.
Cacao, per lb 2
Camomile flowers .... Free

Camphor, crude .... **Free**

       refined, per lb 5

Cantharides .... **Free**

Carboys ....31½ p. c.

Cards, blank..31½ p. c.

       playing, costing not over 25 cents per pack, per pack..........22½ p. c.

       playing, costing over 25 cents per pack, per pack.............31½ p. c.

       printed picture...25 p. c.

       wool and cotton, part iron.............................. ......31½ p. c.

       wool and cotton, part steel....................................40½ p. c.

Carpets, Aubusson and Axminster......................................45 p. c.

       woven whole for rooms.......................................45 p. c.

       Brussels, printed, per square yard............................. 45

       Brussels, tapestry, per square yard............25 1-5 cts. and 31½ p. c.

       Brussels, by Jacquard machine, per sq. yard, 39 3-5 cents and 31½ p. c.

       felt, classed as drugget, per square yard.......22½ cents and 31½ p. c.

       hemp or jute, per square yard....................................... 8

       Saxony, Wilton, and Tournay velvet, by Jacquard machine, per

          square yard,..............................63 cents and 31½ p. c.

       treble ingrain, three-ply, and worsted chain Venetian, per sq.

          yard...................................15 3-10 cents and 31½ p. c.

       velvet; patent and tapestry, printed on the warp or otherwise,

          per square yard...............................36 cents and 31½ p. c.

       yarn Venetian and two-ply ingrain, per sq. yd. 10 4-5 cts. and 31½ p. c.

       wool or cotton, or parts of either, not otherwise provided for, 36 p. c.

       flax....................................... ....40 p. c.

       mats, rugs, etc..40½ p. c.

Castings of iron, not otherwise provided for.........................27 p. c.

Casks and barrels, empty, sugar boxes, shooks, and packing boxes of wood 30 p. c.

Cassia and cassia vera, per lb 10

       buds and ground, per lb.. 20

Castor, or castoreum .... **Free**

Catechu, or cutch... **Free**

Catgut or whipgut, unmanufactured...................................... **Free**

            manufactured .... **Free**

Cenne oil, per gallon.. 30

Chains, as jewelry..25 p. c.

       cable, or parts thereof, per lb.................................... 2¼

       cable, only fit for remanufacture, per ton...................... 7 20

       curb, polished as saddlery...................................31½ p. c.

       fence, halter, trace, and other, not less than ¼ inch in diameter,

          per lb.................................... .... 2¼

       ditto, less than ¼ inch in diameter, per lb.................2 7-10 cents.

       ditto, under No. 9 wire gauge................................31½ p. c.

       hair... 35 p. c.

       watch, silk... 60 p. c.

Chalk, unmanufactured... **Free**

Champagne, and all other sparkling wines, in bottles, per dozen bottles,

       containing each not more than one quart, and more than one pint.... 6 00

Champagne, per dozen bottles, containing not more than one pint each,

       and more than one half pint...................................... 3 00

Champagne, per dozen bottles, containing each one half pint or less.... 1 50

Champagne, in bottles, containing more than one quart, in addition to $6

       per dozen bottles, for each gallon in excess of one quart per bottle ... 2 00

Charcoal .... Free
Chessmen and chess balls, ivory or bone............................ 45 p. c.
        if wood.. 35 p. c.
Chicory root, ground or unground, per lb 1
Chlorate of potash, per lb 3
Chocolate, per lb 5
Cinnamon, per lb 20
Citrate of lime... Free
Clay, China, as kaolino, per ton.. 5 00
        unwrought, pipe and fire clay, per ton........................ 4 50
Cliffstone.. Free
Cloth, bolting... Free
        floor, of cork, India-rubber, etc................................. 45 p. c.
        grass... 30 p. c.
        hemp, manila... 20 p. c.
        India-rubber.. 31½ p. c.
        seersucker, so styled.. 50 p. c.
        waterproof, not otherwise provided for........................ 40½ p. c.
Clothing, ready-made, linen.. 35 p. c.
                of silk, or silk chief value........................ 60 p. c.
                and wearing apparel of every description, made
                up or manufactured wholly or in part by the
                tailor, seamstress, or manufacturer........... 31½ p. c.
Cloves, per lb... 5
        stems, per lb 3
Coal, anthracite .... Free
        bituminous, per ton of 28 bushels, of 80 lbs. to the bushel 75
Coal, slack or culm, which will pass through a half inch screen, per ton 40
Cocculus indicus... Free
Cocoa, per lb 2
        leaves or shells.. Free
        and chocolate, ground or prepared, per lb..................... 5
Cocoanuts .... Free
        oil .... Free
Coffee, of all kinds.. Free
        extracts of.. 20 p. c.
Coir, and coir yarn .... Free
Collections of antiquity, not for sale .... Free
Colocynth .... Free
Columbo root... Free
Combs of all kinds... 31½ cents
Conium, cicuta, or hemlock, seed and leaf............................ Free
Copal gum .... Free
Copper, manufactures of, and copper bottoms....................... 40½ p. c.
        in plates, bars, pigs, etc., per lb............................... 4½
        old, for remanufacture, per lb.................................. 3 3-5 cents
        taken from American bottoms in foreign ports................ Free
        ore, per lb.. 2 7-10 cents
        regulus of, for each pound of fine copper, per lb............. 3 3-5 cents
        sulphate of, per lb.. 4
Copperas, per lb.. 9-20
Cordials, per proof gallon 2 00
Coriander seeds.. Free
Corks and cork bark, manufactured, ad valorem...................... 30 p. c.

Cork bark, unmanufactured.. Free
    wood, unmanufactured.. Free
Corsets, or cloth cut to be made into them, when valued at $6 per dozen,
    per dozen... 2 00
Corsets, when valued at more than $6 per dozen, ad valorem...........35 p. c.
Cotton, raw.. Free
Cotton thread, yarn warps or warp yarn, single or twisted, not wound
    on spools, in whatever form, valued per pound at not more than 40
    cents, per lb.. 6
Cotton valued between 40 and 60 cents per pound, per lb.., ... 18
Cotton thread or warp, valued between 60 and 80 cents, per lb......... 30
Cotton valued at more than 80 cents per pound, per pound............. 60
    In addition to these specific duties, an ad valorem tax of 20 per cent.
Cotton, manufactures of, except as follows....................31½ p. c.
Cottons (except jeans, denims, bed tickings, ginghams, plaids, cotton-
    ades, pantaloons stuff, and goods of like description), not exceeding
    100 threads to the square inch, counting the warp and filling, and ex-
    ceeding in weight 5 ounces per square yard:
    if unbleached, per square yard... 4½
    if bleached, per square yard.....................................4 19-20 cents
    if colored, stained, painted, or printed, per sq. yard...4 19-20 cents and 9 p. c.
    As above, if weighing less than 5 ounces per square yard:
    if unbleached, per square yard.. 2¼
    if bleached, per square yard.....................................2 7-10 cents
    if printed, colored, painted or stained, per square yard .. 3 3-20c. and 9 p. c.
    On finer and lighter goods of light description, not exceeding 200
    threads to the square inch, counting in the warp and filling:
    if unbleached, per square yard.. 4½
    if bleached, per square yard.....................................4 19-20 cents
    if colored, stained, painted, or printed, per sq. yard..4 19-20 cents and 13 p. c.
    on goods of like description, exceeding 200 threads to the square inch,
    counting the warp and filling: If unbleached, per square yard....... 4½
    if bleached, per square yard.....................................4 19-20 cents
    if colored, stained, painted, or printed, per sq. yard.4 19-20 cents and 13 p. c.
Cottons, viz.: jeans, denims, drillings, bed-ticking, ginghams, plaids, cot-
    tonades, pantaloons stuffs, and goods of like description, or for similar
    uses, and not exceeding 100 threads to the square inch, counting warp
    and filling, and exceeding 5 ounces to the square yard. If unbleached,
    per square yard...5 2-5 cents
    if bleached, per square yard.....................................5 17-20 cents
    if colored, stained, pained, or printed, per sq. yard....5 17-20 cents and 9 p. c.
    on finer or lighter goods of like description, not exceeding 200 threads
    to the square inch, counting the warp and filling. If unbleached, per
    square yard..5 2-5 cents
    if bleached, per square yard.....................................5 17-20 cents
    if colored, stained, painted, or printed, per sq. yd..5 17-20 cents and 13½ p. c.
    on goods of lighter description, exceeding 200 threads to the square in.,
    counting warp and filling. If unbleached, per square yard......6 3-10 cents
    if bleached, per square yard... 6¾
    if colored, stained, painted, or printed, per sq. yard....6¾ cts. and 13½ p. c.
    on plain woven cotton goods, not included in the foregoing schedule, if
    unbleached, valued at over 16 cents per square yard................31½ p. c.
    if bleached, valued at over 20 cents per square yard................31½ p. c.
    if colored, stained, painted or printed, valued at over 25c. per sq. yd., 31½ p. c.

Cottons, jeans, denims, and drillings, valued at over 20c. per square yard,
    unbleached...31½ p. c.
    all other cotton goods of every description, the value of which shall
    exceed 25 cents per square yard.......................................31½ p. c.
Cotton, thread of, on spool, containing on each spool not exceeding 100
    yards of thread, per doz.....................................5 2-5 cents and 27 p. c.
    exceeding 100 yards, for every additional 100 yards or fractional part
    thereof, in excess of 100 yards, per doz...............5 2-5 cents and 31½ p. c.
Cotton bagging, or bagging of any other material that may serve the
    same purpose, valued at 7 cents or less per square yard, per lb............ 2
    ditto, when valued at more than 7 cents per square yard, per lb...... 3
Cotton seed oil, per gallon... 30
Cowage down... Free
Cow hair, not cleaned and dressed...................................... Free
Cow or kine pox or vaccine virus.. Free
Cowrie, gum... Free
Cubebs.. Free
Cubic nitre... Free
Cudbear... Free
Cummin seeds... Free
Currants, Zante and other, per lb 1
Curry and curry powders.. Free
Cuttle-fish bone.. Free
Cyanite or Kyanite.. Free
Damar, gum... Free
Dates, per lb... 1
Diamond dust, or bort... Free
Diamonds, rough or uncut, including glaziers' diamonds................ Free
Dolls, copper chief value...40½ p. c.
    wholly or part wool, per lb.........................45 cts. and 31½ p. c.
    of all kinds, except as above.....................................35 p. c.
Dominoes...31½ p. c.
    if toys...45 p. c.
Downs, all descriptions, for beds or bedding........................... Free
Draughts, bone or ivory.. 45 p. c.
Drawings... 20 p. c.
Dress goods, women's and children's, and real or imitation Italian cloths,
    composed wholly or in part of wool, worsted, the hair of the alpaca
    goat, or other like animals, valued at not above 20 cents per square
    yard, per square yard..............................5 2-5 cents and 31½ p. c.
    valued at above 20 cts. per sq. yd., per sq. yard ....7 1-5 cents and 36 p. c.
    weighing 4 oz. and over per sq. yard, per lb...........45 cents and 31½ p. c.
Dried bugs, dried blood, and dried and prepared flowers,.............. Free
Duck, cotton... 27 p. c.
East India gum... Free
Earth, Fuller's, per ton... 2 70
Eggs... Free
Elecampane root.. Free
Embroideries, articles embroidered with gold, silver, or other metal, ex-
        cept copper be a component part of chief value..........31½ p. c.
        cottons, used as balmorals, per lb ....21 3-5 cts. and 31½ p. c.
        wool covers, per lb......................45 cents and 31½ p. c.
        part wool, if clothing, per lb.................45 cents and 36 p. c.

Embroideries, manufactures of cotton and worsted, if embroidered or
    tamboured in the loom or otherwise, by machinery or
    with the needle, or other process, not otherwise provid-
    ed for..31 p. c.
    as above, if linen or silk, if silk not chief value...........35 p. c.
Emery, ore or rocks, not pulverized or ground, per ton..................6 00
Emery grains, per lb..2
Ergot..Free
Esparto, or Spanish grass, and other grasses and pulp of, for the manu-
    facture of paper..Free
Etchings for societies, etc., and not for sale.........................Free
Eyelets of every description, per 1,000...............................6
Farina...Free
Fashion plates engraved on steel or on wood, colored or plain..........Free
Feathers, ostrich, cock, vulture, and other ornamental feathers, crude or
    not dressed, colored, or manufactured...........................25 p. c.
    when dressed, colored, or manufactured.........................50 p. c.
    for beds or bedding...Free
    artificial and ornamental, or parts thereof, of whatever mate-
    rial composed, not otherwise provided for......................50 p. c.
Feeding bottles, glass and India-rubber................................36 p. c.
Fennel seeds...Free
Fonugreek seeds..Free
Fibrin in all forms..Free
Figs, per lb...2½
File, or gespinst..25 p. c.
Files, file blanks and rasps, all kinds, not over 10 inches in length, per
    lb...9 cts. and 27 p. c.
    over 10 inches in length, per lb.................5 2-5 cts. and 27 p. c.
Fire-arms..31½ p. c.
Fire crackers, per box of 40 packs.....................................1 00
Firewood...Free
Fish, fresh, for immediate consumption.................................Free
Fish, fresh, for bait..Free
Fish glue, or isinglass..Free
Fish joints, wrought iron, per lb......................................1 4-5 cents
Fish oil, per gallon...20 p. c.
Flannels, plaid and shirting, per lb..................45c. and 31½ p. c.
Flat-irons, or sad irons, of cast iron, per lb.........................1 7-20 cents
Flaxseed, per bushel of 56 lbs...20
    oil, per gallon..30
Flax straw, per ton..5 00
    not hackled or dressed, per ton....................................20 00
    hackled, known as dressed line, per ton............................40 00
    tow of, per ton..10 00
Flint..Free
Flint stones, ground...Free
Flocks, wool, or pulverized wool, per lb...............................11¼
Flowers, artificial and ornamental, parts thereof, of whatever material
    composed, not otherwise provided for...........................50 p. c.
    dried and prepared as artificial...................................Free
    leaves, plants, roots, barks, and seeds, for medicinal purposes,
    crude, not otherwise provided for..............................Free
    used in dyeing...Free

Flowers, all other not otherwise provided for........................ 10 p. c.
Flues, steam, gas, and water, wrought iron, per lb................... 2½
Foil, gold or silver... 36 p. c.
   tin.. 57 p. c.
   copper, chief value, and for fencing............................ 40½ p. c.
Fossils... Free
Fringes, silk.. 'G p. c.
   other, according to material.
Fruit juice... 25 p. c.
   pie.. 35 p. c.
   green, ripe, or dried, not otherwise provided for.............. 10 p. c.
   pickled... 35 p. c.
   preserved in their own juice... 25 p. c.
   comfits or sweetmeats, preserved in sugar, brandy, or molasses,
     not otherwise provided for...................................... 35 p. c.
   plants, tropical and semi-tropical, for purposes of propagation or
     cultivation... Free
   shade, lawn, and ornamental trees, shrubs, plants, and flower
     seeds, not otherwise provided for............................ 20 p. c.
Furniture, cabinet or household, in piece or rough.................. 30 p. c.
   cabinet wares and house furniture, finished...................... 35 p. c.
   tops for, of composition or scagliola............................... 35 p. c.
   slate tops for.. 40 p. c.
   marble tops for... 50 p. c.
Gallic and tannic acids, per lb... 1 00
Galloons, cotton... 31½ p. c.
   silk.. 60 p. c.
Galanga, or galangal, and garacino.................................... Free
Gentian root... Free
German silver, manufactured... 36 p. c.
      albata, or argentine, unmanufactured................... 31½ p. c.
Gilt ware and plated, all kinds... 31½ p. c.
Gimlets, as manufactures of steel....................................... 40½ p. c.
Gimps, cotton... 31½ p. c.
   silk.. 60 p. c.
Ginger root.. Free
   ground, per lb.. 3
   preserved or pickled, and essence of.............................. 35 p. c.
Ginsing root... Free
Glass, fluted, rolled, or rough plate, not including crown, cylinder or
   common window glass:
   not above 10x15 inches square, per sq. foot.................... 27-40 cent
   above 10x15, and not above 16x24, per square foot............ 9-10 cent
   above 16x24, and not above 24x30, per square foot........... 1 7-20 cents
   all above 24x30, per square foot................................... 1 4-5 cents
   all fluted, rolled, or rough plate glass, weighing over 100 lbs. per
   100 square feet, shall pay an additional duty on the excess at the
   same rates above imposed.
   all cast polished plate glass, unsilvered, not above 10x15 inches
     square, per square foot... 2 7-10 cents
   above 10x15, and not above 16x24, per square foot........... 4½
   above 16x24, and not above 24x30, per square foot........... 7 1-5 cents
   above 24x30, and not above 24x60, per square foot........... 22½
   all above 24x60, per square foot................................... 45

Glass, all cast polished plate glass, silvered, or looking-glass plates:
  not above 10x15 inches square, per square foot................3 3-5 cents
  above 10x15, and not above 16x24, per square foot............5 2-5 cents
  above 16x24, and not above 24-30, per square foot................ 9
  above 24x30, and not above 24x60, per square foot............... 31½
  all above 24x60, per square foot................................ 54
  Provided, that no looking-glass plates or plate glass, silvered, when
  framed, shall pay a less rate of duty than imposed on glass of
  like description not framed, but shall pay in addition 30 per ct.
  upon such frames.
  on all unpolished cylinder, crown, and common window glass, not
    above 10x15 inches square, per square foot ....1 7-20 cents
  above 10x15, and not above 16x24, per square foot............1 4-5 cents
  above 16x24, and not above 24x30, per square foot............... 2¼
  all above 24x30, per square foot............................2 7-10 cents
  cylinder and crown glass, polished, not above 10x15 inches square,
    per square foot.. 2¼
  above 10x15, and not above 16x24, per square foot............3 3-5 cents
  above 16x24, and not above 24x30, per square foot............5 2-5 cents
  above 24x30, and not above 24x60, per square foot............... 18
  all above 24x60, per square foot............................... 36
  colored, for manufacture of buttons and imitation of precious
    stones... 36 p. c.
  broken in pieces, which cannot be cut for use, and fit only for re-
    manufacture... Free
  manufactures, plain and mold and press glass, not cut, engraved,
    or painted...31½ p. c.
  manufactures, cut, engraved, painted, colored, printed, stained,
    silvered, or gilded (not including plate glass silvered or looking-
    glass plates), or of which glass shall be a component material,
    not otherwise provided for................................... 36 p. c.
  porcelain and Bohemian, cut or not............................ 36 p. c.
Globes, wood and iron...31½ p. c.
Gloves, cotton, lined with wool waste, per lb............45 cents and 31½ p. c.
  cotton, edged at the wrist with a small stripe or stripes of color-
    ed worsted yarn, knit for the purpose of ornament..........31½ p. c.
  kid, or other leather... 50 p. c.
  woolen cloth, per lb......................................45 cents and 36 p. c.
Gold, bullion and dust... Free
  leaf, package of 500 leaves, per package...................... 1 35
  manufactures of, not otherwise provided for................... 36 p. c.
  ore, and sweepings of... Free
  size .... 36 p. c.
Goldbeaters' molds, and skins................................. Free
Goods, ware, and merchandise of growth or produce of countries east of
  the Cape of Good Hope (except wool, raw cotton, and raw silk as reeled
  from the cocoon, or not further advanced than train, thrown, or organ-
  zine), when imported from places west of the Cape of Good Hope, in
  addition to the duties on such articles when imported from the place
  or places of their growth or production...................... 10 p. c.
Gouges, as manufactures of steel...............................40½ p. c.
Grease... 10 p. c.
  for use as soap stock only, not otherwise provided for........ Free
Gridirons, as manufactures of iron.............................31½ p. c.

Gunny bags and gunny cloth, valued at ten cents or less per sq. yd..... 40 p. c.
    valued at over 10 cents per sq. yard...... 40 p. c.
    old or refuse, fit only to be remanufact'd.   Free
Guns or muskets...31½ p. c.
   barrel moulds, steel, not in bars.....................40½ p. c
   bayonets, and locks for...............................40 p. c.
Gun wads, all sporting ....31½ p. c.
Gut-cord and worm-gut,....................................... Free
Guts.. Free
Gutta percha, crude...................................... Free
   manufactures of ....36 p. c.
Hackles, part steel ....40½ p. c.
Hair cloth, not otherwise provided for.....................30 p. c.
   of the description known as hair seating, 18 inches wide or
    over, per square yard....................................... 40
   less than 18 inches wide, per square yard.................... 30
   known as crinoline cloth ....30 p. c.
Hair, of horse and cattle, cleaned, but unmanufactured................ Free
   as above, all other kinds, not otherwise provided for............. 10 p. c.
   hog, curled for beds or mattresses, unfit for bristles,............... Free
   of other kinds, curled for beds or mattresses...................... 20 p. c.
   all kinds, uncleaned and unmanufactured .... Free
   horse and cow, not cleaned and dressed.......................... Free
   hogs', per lb.. 1
   manufactures of, not otherwise provided for...................... 50 p. c.
   horse or cattle, cleaned or uncleaned, drawn or undrawn, but un-
    manufactured.. Free
   human, raw, uncleaned, and not drawn............................ 20 p. c.
   human, cleaned or drawn, but not manufactured.................. 30 p. c.
   human, when manufactured....................................... 40 p. c.
Hammers, blacksmiths', per lb..................................... 2¼
   brass or iron...31¼ p. c.
   part steel..40½ p. c.
Hat bodies, cotton...31¼ p. c.
   wool, per lb....................................45 cents and 31½ p. c.
Hatchets, as manufactures of steel................................40½ p. c.
Hatters' irons, of cast-iron, per lb...............................1 7-20 cents
Heading blocks, rough hewn or sawed only.........................20 p. c.
Hellebore root.. Free
Hide cuttings, raw, with or without the hair, for glue stock............. Free
Hides, raw and unmanufactured, all kinds, except sheep with wool on.. Free
Hide rope .... Free
Hinges, wrought or cast iron, per lb................................. 2¼
   other, according to material.
Hoes, iron...31¼ p. c.
   part steel, or steeled...40½ p. c.
Hollow-ware, tinned or glazed, embracing castings of iron only, per lb., 3 3 20c.
Hones.. Free
Hooks, fish. ....40½ p. c.
   and eyes, according to material.
   reaping...40½ p. c.
   iron...31¼ p. c.
Hoops, per lb... 5
Hop roots, for cultivation... Free

Horns, manufactures of...31½ p. c.
    strips.. Free
    and horn tips .... Free
Hubs for wheels, rough-hown or carved only............................ 20 p. c.
Hydrometers, part glass...36 p. c.
India-rubber, crude, and milk of, and in strips, unmanufactured......... Free
    manufactures of, not otherwise provided for............31½ p. c.
Indian hemp (crude dry)... Free
India or Malacca joints, not further advanced than cut into suitable
   lengths for the manufactures into which they are intended to be con-
   verted.. Free
Inkstands, according to material.
Instruments and apparatus, surgeons' and mathematical, according to
    material.
      philosophical... 36 p. c.
Insulators, for use exclusively in telegraphy, except those made of glass, 25 p. c.
Ividium... Free
Iron, acetate of, per lb.. 25
    in pigs, per ton.. 6 70
    cast, scrap, of every description, per ton 5 40
    wrought scrap iron of every description, per ton............... 8 10
    Nothing shall be deemed scrap iron except waste or refuse iron
    that has been in actual use, and fit only to be remanufactured.
    round, in coils, 3-16 of an inch or less in diameter, whether coated
    with metal or not so coated, and all descriptions of iron wire,
    and wire of which iron is a component part, not otherwise spo-
    cifically enumerated and provided for, shall pay the same duty
    as iron wire, bright, coppered, or tinned.
Istic, or Tampico fibre, manufactures of, not suitable for cotton bagging, 30 p. c.
Ivory, and vegetable ivory, unmanufactured,............................ Free
    manufactures of, not otherwise provided for, 31½p.c.
Jackets, woolen, per lb..................................45 cents and 36 p. c.
    cardigan, per lb.................................45 cents and 31½ p. c.
Jalap... Free
Japanned wares, all kinds, not otherwise provided for.................. 36 p. c.
Josstick, or josslight .... Free
Jute, per ton.. 15 00
    buts.. Free
    manufactures of, not otherwise provided for.................... 30 p. c.
Kettles, cast iron, per lb..1 7-20 cents
    other (according to material).
Keys, watch, gold and silver..22½ p. c.
Knives, butcher, bread, bowie, budding, cooks', farriers', fruit, pruning,
    shoe, and table, as cutlery...................................31½ p. c.
    beam, curriers', drawing, fleshers, hay, putty, straw, and tan-
    ners', as manufactures of steel ....40½ p. c.
    pen, jacket, and pocket....................................... 45 p. c.
Labels, blank...22½ p. c.
    printed and figured paper .... 25 p. c.
Lacquered ware...31½ p. c.
Lappets, cotton, per lb.............................21 3-5 cents and 31½ p. c.
Laces, cotton ....31½ p. c.
    silk, and silk and cotton, known as silk lace.................. 60 p. c.
    other, (according to material).

Last blocks..20 p. c.
Laths, hewn and sawed, per 1,000 pieces.............................. 15
Lead, brown acetate of, per lb...................................... 5
    white acetate of, per lb.................................... 10
    ashes of... 9 p. c.
    black, or plumbago... Free
    black, powder, or British luster .... 18 p. c.
    dross, as ore, old scrap, for remanufacture, and ore of, per lb..1 7-20 cents
    pigs and bars, and molted, old bullets, etc., per lb.......1 4-5 cents
    sheets, pipe, or shot, per lb.............................2 19-40 cents
    manufactures of, not otherwise provided for............... 31½ p. c.
    nitrate of, and white or red, per lb......................2 7-10 cents
    sugar of, as acetate of.
Leather, bend, or belting, and Spanish or other sole leather .... 15 p. c.
    calf skins, tanned, or tanned and dressed .... 25 p. c.
    upper, all other kinds.................................... 20 p. c.
    japanned, patent, or enameled, and manufactures of, not other-
      wise provided for.......................................31½ p. c.
    old, scrap.. Free
Leaves, medicinal, crude, and all not otherwise provided for......... Free
Licorice, paste, per lb... 9
    juice, per lb... 4½
    root .... Free
Lime,... 10 p. c.
    acetate, or pyrolignite of................................ 25 p. c.
    chloride, or chlorate of, borate of, and citrate of ...... Free
    hydrocarbonate of, per lb................................. 1
    sulphate of .... 20 p. c.
Linseed, cake (oil-cake) .... Free
    meal .... 20 p. c.
Lint, cotton .... 31½ p. c.
    linen .... 40 p. c
Lithographic stones, not engraved................................... Free
Loadstones.. Free
Locks, brass or iron.. 31½ p. o
    with steel springs.. 40½ p. c
Logs, and round, unmanufactured timber, not otherwise provided for,
    and ship timber... Free
Lumber, sawed boards, planks, deals, and other lumber of hemlock,
    whitewood, sycamore, and basswood, per M.................. 1 00
    same, if planed or finished, $1 per M., and for each side planed
    or finished, per M.. 50
    same, if planed on one side, and tongued or grooved, per M.... 2 00
      two sides, and tongued or grooved, per M.. 2 80
    all other varieties of sawed lumber, per M................ 2 00
    same, if planed on one side, and tongued or grooved, per M.... 3 00
      two sides, and tongued or grooved, per M.. 3 50
    hubs for wheels, posts, last, wagon, oar, and all like blocks,
    rough hewn or sawed only.................................. 20 p. c.
    all timber, squared and sided, not otherwise provided for, per
    cubic foot.. 1
    pickets and palings....................................... 20 p. c.
    shingles, per M... 35
    clapboards, pine, per M................................... 2 00
      spruce, per M... 1 50

Machinery, according to material, except as here specified for manufacture of beet sugar only, and for repairs for same (under regulations); machinery and apparatus for a term of two years after the passage of this act, and no longer, designed only for and adapted to be used for steam towage on canals, and not now manufactured in the United States, imported by any State, or by any person duly authorized by the Legislature of any State (under regulations), and also steam-plow machinery, adapted to the cultivation of the soil, imported by any person for his own use (under regulations)..................... Free
Maccaroni and vermicelli.. Free
Madder and Indi, or munjeet, ground or prepared, and all extracts of... Free
Magnets... Free
Manganese, oxide and ore of.. Free
Marrow, crude.. Free
    for toilet soap, perfumed.....................................50 p. c.
Marsh mallows.. Free
Matico leaf.. Free
Mats, cocoanut, flags, jute, or grass...........................30 p. c.
    India-rubber...40½ p. c.
    palm leaf..35 p. c.
    wool-lining, per lb.....................45 cents and 31½ p. c.
Meal, corn...10 p. c.
    oat, per lb..½
Meerschaum, crude or raw... Free
Metals, bell, broken bells, and pewter and Britannia, old, fit only for
    remanufacture.. Free
    bronze and Dutch, in leaf...................................9 p. c.
    sheathing, or yellow, and sheathing zinc...................2 7-10 cents
    palladium.. Free
    sheathing brass, old, and fit only for remanufacture..........13½ p. c.
    silver-plated, in sheets, or other form......................31½ p. c.
    manufactured, or unmanufactured, not otherwise provided for...18 p. c.
Mica and mica ware... Free
Mill irons, and cranks of wrought iron.........................1 4-5 cents
Milk, preserved or condensed..................................20 p. c.
    sugar of.. Free
Mineral waters, all not artificial..................................... Free
Models of inventions and improvements in the arts..................... Free
Moss, Iceland, and for beds and bedding, and crude.................... Free
    prepared, as artificial flowers............................50 p. c.
Mundic, iron pyrites, or arsenical pyrites....................18 p. c.
    copper pyrites, per lb...4½
Murexide (a d c)... Free
Musk, crude.. Free
    as perfume...50 p. c.
Mustard, in glass or tin, per lb...............................14
    ground, in bulk, per lb......................................10
    seed, brown, and white................................. Free
Nails, board, wrought iron, per lb.............................2¼
    brass, composition, and zinc...............................31½ p. c.
    china heads..40 p. c.
    gold, silver, and German silver............................36 p. c.
    iron, cut, per lb.....................................1 7-20 cents
    horseshoe, per lb...4½

Needles, for sewing, darning, knitting, and other descriptions.........22½ p. c.
    for knitting or sewing machines, per M...........90 cents and 31½ p c.
Nickel, per lb....................... 27
    oxide, and alloy with copper, per lb............................. 18
Nuts, all kinds, not otherwise provided for, per lb..................... 2
    Brazil, or cream, and cocoa.............. ... . Free
Nux vomica... Free
Oilcloths, for floors, stamped, painted, or printed, valued at 50 cents or
    less per square yard..31½ p. c.
    valued at over 50 cents per square yard....................40½ p. c.
    silk...54 p. c.
    all other...40½ p. c.
Oils, all expressed, not otherwise provided for............................20 p. c.
    almonds, mace, and poppy .... Free
    bay, and laurel, per lb.. 20
    castor, mustard salad, olive in flasks or bottles, and salad, olive for
      perpetual lamp in synagogue, each, per gal., and croton, per lb.. 1 00
    mustard, not salad, and olive, not salad, per gal.................... 25
Oils, all essential, not otherwise provided for .... 50 p. c.
    almonds, amber, ambergris. anise, anthos, or rosemary, bergamot,
    cajeput, caraway, cassia, camomile, cinnamon, citronella, or lem-
    on grass, civet, fennel, jasmine, or jessamine, juglandium, juniper.
    lavender, origanum, roses, sesam, thyme, and valerian........... Free
    bay leaves, per lb... 17 50
    cloves, per lb.. 2 00
    cognac, or œnauthic ether, per oz............................. 4 00
    cubebs, per lb.. 1 00
    lemons, and orange, per lb., and rum, or essence of, and bay-rum,
      or essence of, per oz.. 50
Olives, green or prepared, and orchill, weed or liquid.............. .... Free
Ore, specimens of, not otherwise provided for............................ 5 p. c.
Orange buds and flowers, orpiment, osmium, and oxidizing paste........ Free
Paintings, on glass or glasses...36 p. c.
    same, for churches... Free
Paper, all kinds, excepting printing paper, not otherwise provided for, 31½ p.c.
    manufactures of, excepting books and other printed matter....31½ p. c.
    printing, unsized, used exclusively for books and newspapers.... 20 p. c.
    all sized or glued, fit only for printing............................ 25 p. c.
    sheathing... 9 p. c.
    stock, crude, of every description, not otherwise provided for .... Free
Papers, illustrated or not................................. 25 p. c.
Parchment................ .... 27 p. c.
Paste, and pebbles, Brazil, and pebbles for spectacles, rough............ Free
Pellitory root... Free
Pens, metallic, per gross.................. 9 cents and 22½ p. c.
Percussion caps.. 40 p c.
Peruvian bark, phanglein, and pineapple slips, for seed................. Free
Pins, hair, of iron wire.................................... 45 p. c.
    if jewelry, or imitation of....................................... 25 p. c
    solid head, or other....................................31½ p. c.
Pitch.. 20 p. c.
    Burgundy.. Free
Planes, part steel, and plane irons (steel)......................40½ p. c.
Plates, engraved, of copper ....40½ p. c.

Plates, engraved, of steel, and stereotype plates.......................22½ p. c.
    of wood..25 p. c.
    landscape...36 p. c.
    tin and iron, galvanized or coated with any metal by electric bat-
      teries, per lb.. 2
Platina, unmanufactured... Free
    manufactures of... 36 p. c.
Plows, part steel..40½ p. c.
Plush, hatters', cotton and silk, cotton chief value...................22½ p. c.
Pocket-books, all..32½ p. c.
Polypodium... Free
Potash, acetate of, per lb.. 25
    bichromate of, chlorate of, and chromate of, per lb........... 3
    hydriodate, iodate, and iodide of, per lb..................... 75
    hydrate of, as bicarbonate of soda, per lb.................... 1½
    muriate of.. Free
    prussiate of, yellow, per lb.................................. 5
    prussiate of, red, per lb..................................... 10
Potatoes per bushel... 15
Powder, bronze..18 p. c.
Prunes, per lb... 1
Pulu, vegetable substance for beds.................................... Free
Punches, shoe...40½ p. c.
Quick-grass root.. Free
Quinine, and amorphus of, and other salts of ....45 p. c.
    sulphate of...20 p. c.
Rags, other than wool, paper stock of every description, including all
    grasses, fibres, waste, shavings, clippings, old paper, rope ends,
    waste rope, waste bagging, gunny bags and gunny cloth, old or
    refuse, fit only for the manufacture of paper, and cotton waste,
    whether for paper stock or other purposes...................... Free
    woolen, per lb...10 4-5 cents
    other than as above... 9 p. c.
Railroad chairs, wrought iron, per lb.................................1 4-5 cents
    ties, wood.. Free
Raisins, per lb... 2½
Ratans and reeds, unmanufactured...................................... Free
    manufactured..25 p. c.
Rennets, raw or prepared.. Free
Roncon, or Orleans, and all extracts of............................... Free
Root flour, and all roots not otherwise provided for.................. Free
Saddlery, coach and harness hardware of all kinds, and saddles.......31½ p. c.
Safflower, and extract of... Free
Saffron, and saffron cake .... Free
Sago, and sago flour.. Free
Saint John's beans.. Free
Salep, or saloup.. Free
Salt, in bulk, per 100 lbs.. 8
    in bags, sacks, barrels, or other packages, per 100 lbs....... 12
    rock, per 100 lbs... 18
Salts, Epsom, per lb.. 1
    Glauber, per lb... ½
    Rochelle, per lb.. 5
    and preparations of salts, not otherwise provided for..........20 p. c.

6

Santonine, per lb... 3 00
Sassafras, bark and root,.. Free
Sauerkraut .... Free
Saws, buck, not over 10 inches in length, per doz.........67½ cents and 27 p. c.
    over 10 inches in length, per doz..............90 cents and 27 p. c.
    circular..40½ p. c.
    cross-cut, per lineal foot... 9
    hand, all not over 24 inches in length, per doz.....67½ cents and 27 p. c.
    over 24 inches in length, per doz..............90 cents and 27 p. c.
    mill, pit, and drag, not over 9 inches wide, per lineal foot........ 11¼
    over 9 inches wide, per lineal foot............ 18
Scrapers, part steel...40½ p. c.
Screws, iron (commonly known as wood screws), 2 inches or over in
    length, per lb..7 1-5 cents
    less than two inches in length, per lb......................9 9-10 cents
    bed, per lb.. 2¼
    brass...31½ p. c.
Scythes...40½ p. c.
Seaweed, not otherwise provided for, and for beds or matresses......... Free
Shafts, cast steel ....40½ p. c.
Shawls, silk..60 p. c.
    woolen, per lb...45c. and 31½ p. c.
Shingle bolts .... Free
Shirts, imitation merino...31½ p. c.
    bosoms for, not tamboured, linen .... 40 p. c.
Shovels, iron or brass...31½ p. c.
    part steel...40½ p. c.
Shot; cast iron..27 p. c.
Sickles, iron...31½ p. c.
    part steel ....40½ p. c.
Silver bullion, old silver, ore, and sweepings of........................ Free
    nitrate of, and manufactures of, not otherwise provided for....... 36 p. c.
Soap, stocks .... Free
Soda, acetate of, per lb... 25
    all carbonates of, by whatever name designated, not otherwise
    provided for... 20 p. c.
    sal, and soda ash, per lb... ¼
    bicarbonate, and caustic of, per lb 1½
    carbonate, and silicate of, per lb................................. ½
    hyposulphate of... 20 p. c.
    nitrate of, or cubic nitre.. Free
Spades, iron,...31½ p. c.
    part steel...40½ p. c.
Spectacles, brass..31½ p. c.
    gold and silver..36 p. c.
    part steel...40½ p. c.
Spelter, manufactured in blocks or pigs, per lb..................1 7-20 cents
    in sheets, per lb.. 2¼
    manufactures of...31½ p. c.
Spikes, brass..31½ p. c.
Splice-bars, per lb..1 4-5 cents
Spokeshaves, part steel..40½ p. c.
Springs, wire, spiral, for furniture, per lb..............1 4-5c. and 31½ p. c.
Squares, iron, marked on one side, per lb..............2 7-10c. and 27 p. c.

Squares, all other, of iron and steel, per lb.......................5 2-5c. and 27 p. c.
    brass...31¼ p. c.
Steel, manufactures of, not otherwise provided for....................40½ p. c.
    in bars, billets, coils, ingots, and sheets, valued at 7 cents or less
      per pound, per lb...2 1-40 cents
    valued at above 7c. and not above 11c. per lb., per lb........2 7-10 cents
    valued at above 11c. per pound, per lb............3 3-20 cents and 9 p. c.
    bars, slightly tapered, and casts in coils................................27 p. c.
    blooms, and cast, forgings in the rough.........................40½ p. c.
    in any form, not otherwise provided for, and scrap .... 27 p. c.
    railway bars, per lb.. 1¼
Stones, Ayr, as whetstones... Free
    for polishing.. Free
   whet... Free
Storax or styrax.. Free
Straw, and manufactures of .... Free
Strontia, oxide of, or protoxide of strontium..................... Free
    acetate of, per lb.. 25
    muriate of, and nitrate of..20 p. c.
Strychnia, per oz... 1 00
Suspenders, silk..60 p. c.
    silk and India-rubber..45 p. c.
    woolen, per lb...45 cents and 36 p. c.
    any other material and India-rubber......................31¼ p. c.
Tacks, brads and sprigs, cut : not over 16 oz. to the 1,000, per M........ 2¼
    over 16 oz. to the 1,000, per lb........2 7-10 cents
Talc.. Free
Teas, all kinds... Free
Teazles... Free
Teeth, manufactured...20 p. c.
   unmanufactured... Free
Terra alba, aluminous.. Free
Tentmague, manufactured, in blocks or pigs, per lb..........1 7-20 cents
    in sheets, per lb...2 1-40 cents
    manufactures of...31¼ p. c.
Tica, crude... Free
Tin, in bars, blocks, or pigs, and grain tin........................ Free
    liquor, and nitrate of.. 18 p. c.
    manufactures of, not otherwise provided for...................31¼ p. c.
    muriate of, and oxide of.......................................27 p. c.
    in plates or sheets, and tagger or tenn......................15 p. c.
    roofing, continuous, and fastened together ready for use.........31¼ p. c.
    salts of...27 p. c.
Tires, and parts thereof, for locomotives, per lb....................2 7-10 cents
Toys, whole or part wool ....31¼ p. c.
Trimmings, bead..45 p. c.
    silk and metal, and crape trimmings, silk chief value.......50 p. c.
    silk..60 p. c.
    viz., epaulets, galoons, laces, knots, stars, tassels, tresses,
      and wings, of gold, silver and other metals..............31¼ p. c.
Type metal, new..22½ p. c.
    old, and fit only to be remanufactured...................... Free
Umbrellas, parasols, and sun-shades, silk, and alpaca............... 60 p. c.
    other material .... 45 p. c.

Vegetable substances, used for beds or mattresses... Free

      if used for cordage, not otherwise provided for, per ton........ 15 00

      if not otherwise provided for, per ton,...................$5, and 10 p. c.

Vellum...27 p. c.

Venice turpentine,.. Free

Vessels, cast iron, not otherwise provided for, per pound............1 7-20 cents

Wadding, paper or cotton..31½ p. c.

Wafers... Free

Watches, cases, movements, parts of watches, and watch materials..... 25 p. o.

Watch jewels.. 10 p. c.

Wax, bees, and Japan... 20 p. c.

     Brazilian, bay, Chinese, and myrtle .... Free

     sealing.. 35 p. c.

Whalebone, unmanufactured... Free

     manufactures of .... 35 p. c.

Wicks, cotton..31½ p. c.

Wire, iron, bright, coppered, or tinned, drawn and finished, not more

     than ¼ inch in diameter, not less than No. 16 wire gauge, per lb

                                          1 4-5 cents and 13½ p. c.

     over No. 16, and not over 25, wire gauge, per lb....3 3-20c. and 13½ p. c.

     over No. 25 wire gauge, per lb ....3 3-5c. and 13½ p. c.

Wire, steel, not less than ¼ inch in diameter, valued at 7 cents or less

     per pound, per lb ....2 1-40 cents

     valued at above 7c. and not above 11c, per pound, per lb......2 7-10 cents

     valued at above 11 cents per pound, per lb..........3 2-20 cents and 9 p. c.

Wire, steel less than ¼ inch in diameter, not less than No. 16 wire gauge,

     per lb...2¼ cents and 18 p. c.

     less than No. 16 wire gauge, per lb.............2 7-10 cents and 18 p. c.

     of steel, or steel commercially known as crinoline, corset, and hat

     steel wire, per lb ....8 1-10 cents and 9 p. c.

     springs, wire spiral, for furniture, per lb..........1 4-5 cents and 13½ p. c.

Wool, hair of the alpaca goat, and other like animals, unmanufactured,

     shall be divided, for the purpose of fixing the duties, into three classes:

     classes 1 and 2, clothing and combing wools, hair of the alpaca

     goat, and other like animals, the value whereof at the last port

     or place whence exported into the United States, excluding

     charges in such port, shall be 32 cents or less per pound, per lb.,

                                        9 cents and 9 9-10 p. c.

     exceeding 32 cents per lb., per lb ....10 4-5 cents and 9 p. c.

     class 3, carpet, and all other similar wools, the value whereof at

     the last port or place whence exported into the United States,

     excluding charges in such port, shall be 12c. or less per pound,

     per lb...2 7-10 cents

     exceeding 12 cents per pound, per lb..........................5 2-5 cents

Wool, pickings, per lb................................... 9 cents and 9 9-10 p. c.

     manufactures of, of every description, made wholly or in part of

     wool, not otherwise provided for, woolen cloths, and woolen

     shawls, per lb ....45 cents and 31½ p. c.

Worsted, manufactures of, the hair of the alpaca goat, or other like ani-

     mals of every description, wholly or part of, except such as are com-

     posed in part of wool, not otherwise provided for, and flannels, blank

     ets, hats of wool, knit goods, balmorals, woolen and worsted yarn,

     valued at 40 cents or less per pound, per lb ....18 cents and 31½ p. c.

Worsted, valued at above 40 cents and not above 60 cents per pound, per lb..27 cents and 31½ p. c.
     valued above 60c. and not above 80c. per lb., per lb., 36c. and 31½ p. c.
     valued at above 80 cents per pound, per lb.....35 cents and 31½ p. c.

Yams.. Free
Yarp, coir.. Free
Yeast cakes... Free
Zaffer .... Free
Zinc, acetate of...25 p. c.
     corrugated..31½ p. c.
     manufactured in blocks or pigs, per lb........................1 7-20 cents
     in sheets, per lb...2 1-40 cents
     manufactures of, not otherwise provided for .... 18 p. c.
     old, and fit only to be remanufactured .... 18 p. c.
     oxide of, per lb..1 23-40 cents
     sulphate of ....18 p. c.
     valerianate of..36 p. c.

GOLD AND SILVER COINS.

VALUE OF FOREIGN GOLD AND SILVER COINS IN THE MONEY OF UNITED STATES.

GOLD COINS.			SILVER COINS.		
Country.	Denomination.	Value gold.	Country.	Denomination.	Value Silv'r.
Australia	Pound of 1852 ...	$5 32	Austria	Old rix dollar	$1 02
do	Sovereign, 1855–60....	4 86	do	Old scudo	1 03
Austria	Ducat...............	2 29	do	Florin before 1858 ...	51
do	Sovereign...........	6 75	do	New union dollar ...	73
do	New union crown....	6 64	Belgium	Five francs	98
Belgium	Twenty-five francs..	4 72	Bolivia	New dollar..........	79
Bolivia	Doubloon	15 59	do	Half dollar	39
Brazil	Twenty milreis......	10 91	Brazil	Double milreis	1 03
Central America	Two escudos	3 69	Canada	Twenty cents	19
Chili............	Old doubloon........	15 59	Central America	Dollar	1 00
do	Ten pesos	9 15	Chili	Old dollar	1 07
Denmark	Ten thaler	7 90	do	New dollar...........	98
Ecuador	Four escudos	7 55	Denmark	Two rigsdaler.......	1 11
England........	Pound or sovereign ..	4 86	England	Shilling	23
France	Napoleon or 20 francs	3 86	France	Five francs	98
Germany, North	Ten thaler	7 90	Germany, North	Thaler, before 1857 ...	73
do	Ten thaler, Prussian .	7 97	do	New thaler	73
do	Krone—crown	6 64	Germany, South	Florin, before 1857....	42
do South	Ducat...............	2 28	do	New florin...........	42
Greece	Twenty drachms	3 44	Greece	Five drachms........	48
Hindostan......	Mohur	7 08	Hindostan......	Rupee...............	47
Italy	Twenty lire	3 84	Japan...........	Itzebn	38
Japan..........	Old cobang	4 44	do	New itzebu	34
do	New cobang	3 53	Mexico	Dollar—new	1 07
Mexico	Doubloon	15 61	Naples	Scudo	95
Naples	Six ducati........	5 04	Netherlands ...	Two and ½ guilders ..	1 03
Netherlands ...	Ten Guilders	4 00	Norway	Specie daler	1 11
New Granada ...	Old doubloon, Bogota.	15 61	New Granada ...	Dollar of 1857	98
do	Old doubloon. Popayan	15 32	Peru...........	Old dollar	1 06
do	Ten pesos.	9 68	do	Dollar,-of 1858......	95
Peru	Old doubloon.......	15 56	do	Half-dollar, 1835–38..	38
Portugal	Gold crown	5 81	Prussia	Thaler, before 1857 ...	73
Prussia	New union crown ...	6 64	do	New thaler	73
Rome	Two & one-half scudi	2 60	Rome	Scudo	1 06
Russia	Five roubles	3 98	Russia	Rouble	79
Spain	One hundred reals ..	4 96	Sardinia........	Five lire	98
do	Eighty reals	3 86	Spain	New pistareen.......	1 20
Sweden	Ducat...............	2 24	Sweden	Rix dollar	1 11
Tunis	Twenty-five piastres.	3 00	Switzerland	Two francs	40
Turkey	One hundred piastres.	4 37	Tunis	Five piastres	64
Tuscany	Sequin	2 31	Turkey..........	Twenty piastres	87
			Tuscany........	Florin...............	28

AGRICULTURAL.

SUMMARY FOR EACH STATE, SHOWING THE PRODUCT, THE NUMBER OF
ACRES, AND THE VALUE OF EACH CROP FOR 1870.

STATES.	INDIAN CORN.			WHEAT.		
	Bushels.	Acres.	Value of crop.	Bushels.	Acres.	Value of crop.
Maine	1,198,000	36,303	$1,305,720	264,000	17,837	$409,920
New Hampshire..	1,213,000	33,232	1,322,170	174,000	11,756	276,660
Vermont	1,920,000	48,484	2,112.000	409,000	24,345	666.670
Massachusetts...	1,327,000	40,212	1,300,400	35,000	1,988	61,250
Rhode Island	280,000	10,769	296,800	700	39	1,225
Connecticut......	1,413,000	53,522	1,610,820	38,000	2,134	57,700
New York	19,436,000	571,352	16,900,620	9,133,000	661,811	12,877,520
New Jersey......	10,057,000	304,757	8,146,170	1,680 000	131,250	2,409,400
Pennsylvania....	38,866,000	1,085,642	20,149,500	17,115,000	1,426,250	21,736,050
Delaware........	3,311,000	132,440	2,152,150	626,000	62,600	782,500
Maryland	11,818,000	525,244	8,390,780	4,792,000	494,020	6,133,700
Virginia	19,360,000	968,000	12,584,060	6,705,000	608,437	8,314,200
North Carolina..	22,500,000	1,541,095	17,550,000	4,218,000	490,465	5,103,780
South Carolina...	12,000,000	1,348,314	12,720,000	1,012,000	144,571	1,912,680
Georgia	31,000,000	2,296,296	27,900,000	2,387,000	298,375	3,508,800
Florida	2,247,000	208,055	3,033,450	....	....	....
Alabama	35,334,000	2,019,085	32,860,690	1,041,000	123,928	1,332,480
Mississippi......	30,300,000	1,836,363	29,694,000	221,000	22,763	335,920
Louisiana	18,000,000	800,000	19,800,000	41 000	4,226	62,320
Texas...........	23,690,000	893,962	25,111,400	1,225,000	104,700	2,119,250
Arkansas	25,0000,00	786,163	20,000,000	1,251,000	115,833	1,026,300
Tennessee	51,000,000	1,976,744	23,970,000	7,357,000	836,022	7,136,200
West Virginia...	9,837,000	323,585	6,295,680	2,533,000	222,105	3,090,200
Kentucky	63,345,000	1,073,364	30,405,600	5,610,000	561,000	5,610,000
Missouri	94,990,000	3,025,150	41,765,600	6,730,000	519,230	6,142,500
Illinois..........	201,378,000	5,720,965	70,482,300	27,115,000	2,259,563	25,488,100
Indiana	113,150,000	2,864,556	42,997,000	20,200,000	1,836,363	20,200,000
Ohio	87,751,000	2,250,025	42,120,480	19,150,000	1,387,621	20,873,500
Michigan	19,035,000	514,459	10,469,250	15,288,000	1,092,000	16,511,040
Wisconsin	19,995,000	526,184	10,397,400	20,485,000	1,528,731	18,436,500
Minnesota.......	5,823,000	176,454	2,969,730	16,022,000	1,054,078	13,298,260
Iowa	93,415,000	2,919,218	31,761,100	20,445,000	1,635,600	15,047,100
Kansas	16,685,000	595,892	9,677,300	2,343,000	156,200	2,014,960
Nebraska	5,163,000	172,675	1,858,680	1,848,000	128,333	1,182,720
California	1,099,000	30,870	1,318,800	14,175,000	746,052	15,592,500
Oregon	88,000	2,962	88,000	2,270,000	116,410	2,156,500
Nevada	11,000	314	13,756	251,000	10,680	376,500
The Territories...	1,230,000	34,261	1,217,700	1,675,000	65,175	2,026,750
Total.....	1,094,255,000	38,646,977	$601,839,030	235,884,700	18,992,501	$245,865,045

STATES.	RYE.			OATS.		
	Bushels.	Acres.	Value of crop.	Bushels.	Acres.	Value of crop.
Maine	32,000	1,818	$44,169	2,163,000	78,941	$1,403,950
New Hampshire..	43,000	2,687	53,320	1,086,000	35,892	703,560
Vermont	67,000	4,240	77,050	3,70,000	94,065	1,870,300
Massachusetts...	532,000	15,064	255,200	733,000	27,765	535,090
Rhode Island.....	20,60	1,144	26,162	152,000	4,648	92,720
Connecticut......	289,000	20,069	335,240	913,000	28,179	629,970
New York	2,230,000	171,538	2,163,100	29,646,000	915,000	17,194,680
New Jersey	470,000	35,074	455,900	4,040,000	130,612	2,186,400
Pennsylvania....	3,148,000	262,333	2,801,720	34,249,000	1,051,809	16,458,720
Delaware	10,000	892	8,300	498,000	24,900	249,000
Maryland	264,000	25,142	205,920	3,296,000	136,916	1,544,420
Virginia	519,000	54,002	378,870	7,175,000	367,948	3,013,500

SUMMARY FOR EACH STATE, SHOWING THE PRODUCT, THE NUMBER OF ACRES, AND THE VALUE OF EACH CROP FOR 1870—Continued.

STATES.	RYE.			OATS.		
	Bushels.	Acres.	Value of crop.	Bushels.	Acres.	Value of crop.
North Carolina...	400,000	48,192	$389,000	2,750,000	169,753	1,567,500
South Carolina....	60,000	10,344	105,000	926,000	95,463	777,840
Georgia	100,000	12,345	149,000	1,260,000	86,301	1.045,800
Florida	......	......	......	116,400	9,312	116,400
Alabama	60,000	6,185	63,800	700,000	44,871	553,000
Mississippi	21,000	2,100	34,020	800,000	20,689	270,000
Louisiana	21,000	2,100	34,020	87,000	3,480	65,250
Texas	95,000	4,973	105,450	1,500,000	69,444	1,500,000
Arkansas	41,600	2,285	41,600	671,000	28,432	416,020
Tennessee.........	232,000	20,530	287,920	3,920,000	203,104	1,803,200
West Virginia ...	280,900	19,853	512,400	2,655,000	97,610	1,062,000
Kentucky	790,000	65,289	560,900	6,146,000	265,000	2,459,200
Missouri	299,000	19,166	203,320	5,525,000	221,000	2,044,250
Illinois	2,235,000	136,290	1,341,000	38,502,000	1,490,846	12,320,640
Indiana	517,000	37,737	361,900	11,668,000	415,231	4,083,800
Ohio	450,000	32,606	342,000	24,500,000	787,781	9,310,000
Michigan..........	604,000	33,186	453,000	9,831,000	276,498	3,834,090
Wisconsin	1,219,000	89,632	755,780	14,327,000	513,512	5,587,530
Minnesota	74,000	4,180	41,440	8,959,000	272,310	3,046,060
Iowa	518,000	29,431	300,440	16,340,000	550,168	4,902,000
Kansas	77,500	3,725	53,475	3,688,000	117,079	1,475,200
Nebraska	12,900	544	6,966	1,220,000	36,379	367,800
California	24,900	655	29,631	1,581,000	44,535	932,700
Oregon............	3,800	152	3,306	1,867,000	51,861	858,829
Nevada	300	12	375	59,000	1,815	48,970
The Territories ..	13,000	565	16,120	1,031,000	31,242	804,180
Total.....	15,473,600	1,176,137	$12,612,605	247,277,400	8,792,395	$107,136,710

STATES.	BARLEY.			BUCKWHEAT.		
Maine	586,000	30,051	$340,140	443,000	19,453	$332,250
New Hampshire..	96,000	4,465	102,720	87,000	5,860	79,210
Vermont	107,000	4,592	108,070	336,000	19,200	252,000
Massachusetts ...	126,000	6,086	136,080	38,000	2,704	38,760
Rhode Island	30,000	1,250	28,800	1,400	100	1,428
Connecticut......	24,000	905	24,480	96,000	6,857	100,800
New York	6,616,000	312,075	5,623,600	3,445,000	191,899	2,742,350
New Jersey......	7,000	250	7,700	311,000	12,795	311,000
Pennsylvania....	497,000	20,794	452,270	2,278,000	126,555	1,936,300
Delaware.........	1,700	85	1,564	1,300	65	1,300
Maryland.........	10,700	486	9,630	67,000	4,962	74,370
Virginia	7,000	350	5,600	44,000	2,730	30,800
North Carolina...	2,000	90	1,220	17,800	831	10,324
South Carolina...	7,000	466	6,650	......	......	......
Georgia	12,000	800	11,640	......	......	......
Florida	......	......	......	......	......	......
Alabama	......	......	......	......	......	......
Mississippi	......	......	......	......	......	......
Louisiana	......	......	......	......	......	......
Texas...........	54,000	1,800	71,820	......	......	......
Arkansas	......	......	......	......	......	......
Tennessee	30,800	1,368	23,100	9,500	475	7,125
West Virginia....	56,000	2,800	47,600	77,000	3,869	61,600
Kentucky........	304,000	16,000	319,200	18,000	1,077	13,500
Missouri	285,000	10,795	249,400	84,000	3,559	56,280
Illinois	2,232,000	111,600	1,383,840	206,000	10,957	140,080
Indiana	800,000	33,195	664,000	309,000	16,093	219,300
Ohio	1,578,000	67,149	1,357,080	270,000	16,564	229,500
Michigan	630,000	25,200	504,000	901,000	32,080	558,620
Wisconsin	1,431,000	54,000	958,770	498,000	24,776	262,920
Minnesota.......	980,000	40,000	529,200	53,000	2,849	31,800
Iowa	1,227,000	47,192	773,010	200,000	9,259	132,000
Kansas	92,500	3,854	69,375	31,000	1,504	23,870
Nebraska	233,700	8,053	151,903	2,800	106	3,528
California	7,378,000	274,275	7,230,440	22,500	632	24,075
Oregon...........	202,000	6,253	137,360	1,400	45	1,974
Nevada	324,000	11,781	362,880	900	32	990
The Territories...	328,000	10,860	321,440	1,900	66	1,900
Total.....	26,295,400	1,108,924	$22,244,584	9,841,500	536,992	$7,725,044

SUMMARY FOR EACH STATE, SHOWING THE PRODUCT, THE NUMBER OF
ACRES, AND THE VALUE OF EACH CROP FOR 1870—Continued.

STATES	POTATOES.			TOBACCO.		
	Bushels.	Acres.	Value of crop.	Pounds.	Acres.	Value of crop.
Maine	6,527.000	52,216	$4.307,820	....	...	....
New Hampshire	2,980.000	33,863	2,354,200	150,000	150	$33,000
Vermont	4,899.000	34,992	2,498,490	70,000	66	15,400
Massachusetts	2,208.000	25,090	2,119,680	6,289,000	4,658	1,309,360
Rhode Island	488,000	6,177	478,240	....	.....	....
Connecticut	1,729,000	23,604	1,714,710	7,495,000	5,996	1,693,870
New York	25,121,000	256,336	16,328,650	2,584,000	2,349	516,800
New Jersey	3,859.000	51,440	3,626,520	40,000	34	9,200
Pennsylvania	11,084,000	127,402	8,645,520	3,294,000	2,745	691,740
Delaware	217,000	2,893	217,000	....	......	....
Maryland	897,000	13,388	807,300	14,522,000	22,797	1,248,892
Virginia	1,236,000	22,472	877,560	43,761,000	59,216	3,194,553
North Carolina	742,000	9,160	519,400	30,000,000	51,194	4,230,000
South Carolina	113,000	2,354	129,950	....	......	....
Georgia	350,000	4,487	469,000	....	......	....
Florida	10,000	153	11,500	165,000	242	24,730
Alabama	450,000	6,428	616,500	....	......	....
Mississippi	392,000	5,369	454,720	....	......	....
Louisiana	297,000	2,828	344,520	....	......	....
Texas	400,000	3,125	532,000	....	......	....
Arkansas	450,000	4,128	481,500	2,225,000	3,340	340,425
Tennessee	1,220,000	13,863	634,400	35,000,000	41,420	2,905,000
West Virginia	1,021,000	12,011	592,180	2,292,000	3,015	258,998
Kentucky	1,800,000	23,076	1,134,000	45,000,000	64,655	3,690,000
Missouri	2,200,000	21,359	1,232,000	19,610,000	26,146	1,823,730
Illinois	8,427,000	104,037	5,393 280	5,564,000	6,623	712,192
Indiana	2,565,000	57,000	2,128,950	6,930,000	8,152	367,290
Ohio	8,282.000	115,027	6,702,420	21,100,000	23,034	2,595,300
Michigan	7,000,000	73,684	4,060,000	3,500,000	3,684	700,000
Wisconsin	4,585,000	80,438	3,392,900	1,037,000	1,152	186,660
Minnesota	1,274,000	24,037	1,210,300	....	.....	......
Iowa	4,680,000	49,263	2,433,600	....	.....	......
Kansas	3,139,000	29,613	1,757,840	....	.....	......
Nebraska	769,000	8,180	430,640	....	.....	......
California	1,823,000	12,317	2,461,050	....	.....	......
Oregon	414,000	4,758	318,780	....	.....	......
Nevada	155,000	1,781	245,200	....	.....	......
The Territories	973,000	6,710	963,270	....	.....	......
Total	114,775,000	1,325,119	$82,668,590	250,628,000	330,608	$26,747,158

STATES.	HAY.			STATES.	HAY.		
	Tons.	Acres.	Value of crop.		Tons.	Acres.	Value of crop.
Maine	821,000	1,026,250	$16,165,490	Arkansas	10,200	6,800	$153,000
New Hampsh.	526,000	541,666	10,322,000	Tennessee	155,000	108,391	2,579,200
Vermont	979,000	1,019,791	14,195,500	W. Virgin.	242,000	192,063	2,420,000
Mass	507,000	473,831	13,252,980	Kentucky	160,000	117,647	2,420,000
Rhode Island	89,000	81,651	2,136,000	Missouri	532,000	412,403	6,820,240
Connecticut	433,000	333,076	11,024,900	Illinois	1,895,000	1,605,932	20,352,300
New York	4,491,000	3,651,219	77,290,110	Indiana	972,000	765,354	21,139,120
New Jersey	553,000	395,000	10,730,320	Ohio	1,923,000	1,467,938	11,191,460
Pennsylvania	2,734,000	2,103,076	35,678,700	Michigan	1,472,000	1,082,352	16,442,240
Delaware	37,000	37,000	740,000	Wisconsin	1,223,000	912,686	12,755,890
Maryland	232,000	190,163	3,788,569	Minnesota	724,000	492,517	4,901,480
Virginia	216,000	156,521	3,179,520	Iowa	1,600,000	1,194,029	12,320,000
N. Carolina	169,000	120,714	1,934,430	Kansas	529,000	452,136	3,799,220
S Carolina	74,000	74,000	1,602,840	Nebraska	145,000	103,571	812,000
Georgia	55,000	41,044	1,283,150	California	617,000	416,891	10,303,900
Florida	......	......	....	Oregon	86,000	59,310	1,036,300
Alabama	62,000	46,616	1,240,000	Nevada	40,000	29,029	900,000
Mississippi	39,000	28,467	824,750	Territories	128,000	82,580	2,042,880
Louisiana	35,800	23,866	1,020,300				
Texas	25,000	5,625	384,000	Total	24,525,000	19,261,805	$338,969,680

ESTIMATED QUANTITIES, NUMBER OF ACRES, AND AGGREGATE VALUE OF
THE PRINCIPAL CROPS OF THE FARM IN 1870.

PRODUCTS.	Number of bushels.	Number of acres.	Value.
Indian corn	1,094,255,000	38,646,977	$601,839,030
Wheat	235,884,700	18,992,591	245,865,045
Rye	15,473,600	1,176,137	12,612,605
Oats	247,277,400	8,792,395	107,136,710
Barley	26,295,400	1,108,924	22,244,534
Buckwheat	9,841,500	536,992	7,725,044
Potatoes	114,775,000	1,325,119	82,668,590
Total	1,743,802,600	70,579,135	$1,080,091,608
Tobacco..........pounds..	250,628,000	330,668	$26,747,158
Hay.........................tons..	24,525,000	19,861,805	338,969,680
Cotton..................bales..	4,400,000	8,680,000	246,000,000
Total	....	99,451,608	$1,731,808,446

AVERAGE YIELD AND CASH VALUE, AND PRICE PER BUSHEL, TON OR
POUND, OF FARM PRODUCTS FOR THE YEAR 1870.

PRODUCTS.	Average yield per acre.	Average price per bushel.	Average value per acre.	PRODUCTS.	Average yield per acre.	Av. price per bushel. ton or lb.	Av'rage value pr acre.
Indian corn bu..	28 3	$0 54 9	$15 57	B'kwheat bu..	18 3	$0 78 4	$14 38
Wheat .... " ..	12 4	1 04 2	12 94	Potatoes... " ..	86 6	72	62 38
Rye .... " ..	13 1	81 5	10 72	Tobacco .. lbs..	757	10 6	80 88
Oats........ " ..	28 1	43 3	12 18	Hay.....tons..	1 23	13 82	17 06
Barley .... " ..	23 7	84 5	20 05	Cotton....lbs..	236	14	32 94

AVERAGE YIELD OF FARM PRODUCTS PER ACRE FOR THE YEAR 1870.

STATES.	Corn.	Wheat.	Rye.	Oats.	Barley.	Buck-wheat.	Pota-toes.	Tobac-co.	Hay.
	Bush.	Bush.	Bush.	Bush.	Bush.	Bush.	Bush.	Pounds.	Tons.
Maine	33 0	14 8	17 6	27 4	19 5	24 0	125	......	80
New Hampshire..	36 5	14 8	16 0	29 7	21 5	15 0	82	1,000	96
Vermont	39 6	16 8	15 8	33 7	23 3	17 5	140	1,050	96
Massachusetts ...	33 0	17 6	15 4	26 4	20 7	14 0	88	1,350	1 07
Rhode Island	26 0	17 6	18 0	32 7	24 0	14 0	79	....	1 09
Connecticut	26 4	17 8	14 4	32 4	26 5	14 0	73	1,250	1 30
New York	34 0	13 8	13 0	32 4	21 2	17 9	98	1,100	1 23
New Jersey	33 0	12 8	13 4	31 0	28 0	24 3	75	1,150	1 40
Pennsylvania.....	35 8	12 0	12 0	32 6	29 9	18 0	87	1,200	1 30
Delaware	25 0	10 0	11 2	20 0	20 0	20 0	75	....	1 00
Maryland	22 5	9 7	10 5	24 0	22 0	13 5	67	637	1 22
Virginia	20 0	9 6	9 6	19 5	20 0	16 0	55	739	1 38
North Carolina...	14 6	8 6	8 3	16 2	22 0	21 4	81	586	1 40
South Carolina...	8 9	7 0	5 8	9 7	15 0	....	48	...	1 00
Georgia	13 5	8 0	8 1	14 6	15 0	....	78	...	1 34
Florida	10 8	..		12 5	....	....	75	680	..
Alabama	17 5	8 4	9 7	15 6	....	....	70	...	1 33
Mississippi	16 5	9 7	10 0	14 5	....	....	73	...	1 37
Louisiana	22 5	9 7	10 0	25 0	....	....	105	...	1 50
Texas	26 5	11 7	19 1	21 6	30 0	....	128	...	1 60
Arkansas	31 8	10 8	18 2	23 6	....	....	109	666	1 50
Tennessee	25 8	8 8	11 3	19 3	22 5	20 0	88	845	1 43
West Virginia	30 4	11 4	14 1	27 2	20 0	19 9	85	760	1 26
Kentucky	32 1	10 0	12 1	23 2	19 0	16 7	78	696	1 36
Missouri	31 4	13 0	15 6	25 0	26 4	23 6	103	750	1 29
Illinois	35 2	12 0	16 4	26 0	20 0	18 8	81	840	1 18
Indiana	39 5	11 0	13 7	28 1	24 1	19 2	45	850	1 27
Ohio	39 0	13 8	13 8	31 1	23 5	16 3	72	916	1 31
Michigan	37 0	14 0	18 2	35 3	25 0	17 3	95	950	1 36
Wisconsin	38 0	13 4	13 6	27 9	26 5	20 1	57	900	1 34
Minnesota	33 0	15 2	17 7	32 9	24 5	18 6	53	...	1 47
Iowa	32 0	12 5	17 6	29 7	26 0	21 6	95	...	1 34
Kansas	28 0	15 0	20 8	31 5	24 0	20 6	106	...	1 17
Nebraska	29 9	14 4	23 7	33 7	29 0	26 2	94	...	1 40
California	35 6	19 0	38 0	35 5	26 9	32 5	148	...	1 48
Oregon	29 7	19 5	25 0	36 0	32 3	30 7	87	...	1 45
Nevada	35 0	23 5	24 0	32 5	27 5	27 5	87	...	1 35
The Territories..	35 0	25 7	23 0	23 0	30 2	28 5	145	...	1 55

AVERAGE CASH VALUE OF FARM PRODUCTS PER ACRE FOR THE YEAR 1870.

STATES.	Corn.	Wheat.	Rye.	Oats.	Barley.	Buck-wheat.	Pota-toes.	Tobac-co.	Hay.
Maine	$37 62	$26 34	$24 28	$17 81	$19 30	$18 00	$82 50	....	$15 75
New Hampshire	39 78	23 53	19 84	19 60	23 00	12 45	69 52	$220 00	19 05
Vermont	43 56	27 38	18 17	19 88	23 53	13 12	71 40	231 80	13 92
Massachusetts	32 34	30 80	16 94	19 27	22 35	14 28	84 48	324 00	27 96
Rhode Island	27 56	30 80	22 86	19 94	23 04	14 28	77 42	....	26 16
Connecticut	30 09	27 05	16 70	22 35	27 03	14 70	72 27	282 50	33 28
New York	29 58	19 45	12 61	18 79	18 02	14 49	63 70	220 00	21 16
New Jersey	26 73	18 30	12 99	16 74	30 80	24 30	70 50	264 50	27 21
Pennsylvania	26 85	15 24	10 68	15 64	21 74	15 30	67 86	252 00	16 96
Delaware	16 25	12 50	9 29	10 00	18 40	20 00	75 00	....	20 00
Maryland	15 97	12 41	8 19	11 28	19 80	14 98	60 30	54 78	19 92
Virginia	13 00	11 90	7 00	8 19	16 00	11 20	39 05	53 94	20 31
North Carolina	11 38	10 40	8 05	9 23	13 42	12 41	56 70	82 62	16 05
South Carolina	9 43	13 23	9 86	8 14	14 25	...	55 20	....	21 66
Georgia	12 15	11 76	12 06	12 11	14 55	...	104 52	...	31 28
Florida	14 58	....	....	12 50	...	...	86 25	102 00	....
Alabama	16 27	10 75	10 28	12 32	...	...	95 90	....	26 60
Mississippi	16 17	14 74	16 20	13 05	...	...	84 68	....	29 11
Louisiana	24 75	14 74	16 20	18 75	...	...	121 80	....	42 75
Texas	28 09	20 24	21 20	21 60	39 90	...	170 24	....	24 57
Arkansas	25 44	14 04	18 20	14 63	...	...	116 63	101 89	22 50
Tennessee	12 12	8 53	9 15	8 87	16 87	15 00	45 76	70 13	23 79
West Virginia	19 45	13 90	11 70	10 88	17 00	15 92	49 30	85 88	12 60
Kentucky	15 40	10 00	8 59	9 28	19 95	12 52	49 14	57 07	18 02
Missouri	13 81	11 83	10 60	9 25	22 17	15 81	57 68	69 75	16 53
Illinois	12 32	11 24	9 84	8 32	12 40	12 78	51 84	107 52	12 67
Indiana	15 01	11 00	9 59	9 83	20 00	13 63	37 35	.45 05	14 55
Ohio	18 72	15 04	10 48	·11 81	20 21	13 85	58 32	112 66	14 43
Michigan	20 35	15 12	13 65	13 76	20 00	10 72	55 10	190 00	15 19
Wisconsin	19 76	12 06	8 43	10 88	17 75	10 85	42 18	162 00	13 97
Minnesota	16 83	12 61	9 91	11 18	13 23	11 16	50 35	....	9 95
Iowa	10 88	9 75	10 20	8 91	16 38	14 90	49 40	....	10 31
Kansas	16 24	12 90	14 35	12 60	18 00	15 86	59 36	....	8 40
Nebraska	10 76	9 21	12 79	10 11	18 85	33 01	52 64	....	7 84
California	42 72	20 90	45 22	20 94	26 36	34 77	199 80	....	24 71
Oregon	29 70	18 52	21 75	16 56	22 96	43 28	66 99	....	17 47
Nevada	43 75	35 25	30 00	26 97	30 80	30 25	160 08	....	30 37
The Territories	35 54	31 09	28 52	25 74	29 59	28 50	143 55	....	24 73

TOTAL AVERAGE CASH VALUE PER ACRE OF THE ABOVE CROPS FOR 1870.

STATES.	Aver. val. pr. acre.	STATES.	Aver. val. pr. acre.	STATES.	Aver. val. acre.	STATES.	Aver. val. pr. acre.
Maine	$19 55	Maryland	$15 71	Arkansas	$24 34	Minnesota	$12 59
New Hampsh.	22 76	Virginia	13 55	Tennessee	12 25	Iowa	10 65
Vermont	17 43	N. Carolina	12 87	W. Virginia	16 03	Kansas	13 87
Mass	32 15	S Carolina	10 29	Kentucky	15 00	Nebraska	10 51
Rhode Island	28 94	Georgia	12 54	Missouri	14 17	California	24 82
Connecticut	36 35	Florida	14 63	Illinois	12 03	Oregon	19 03
New York	22 53	Alabama	16 31	Indiana	13 61	Nevada	35 48
New Jersey	26 28	Mississippi	16 50	Ohio	17 03	Territories	31 94
Pennsylvania	18 93	Louisiana	25 49	Michigan	16 96		
Delaware	15 91	Texas	18 12	Wisconsin	·14 13		

ESTIMATED TOTAL NUMBER AND TOTAL VALUE OF EACH KIND OF LIVE STOCK, AND THE AVERAGE PRICE IN FEBRUARY 1871.

STATES.	HORSES.			MULES.		
	Number.	Average price.	Value.	Number.	Average price.	Value.
Maine	83,000	$86 38	$7,169,540	------	-------	------
New Hampshire	49,500	89 29	4,419,855	------	-------	------
Vermont	71,000	97 49	6,921,790	------	-------	------
Massachusetts	99,900	129 89	12,976,011	------	-------	------
Rhode Island	15,300	98 19	1,502,307	------	-------	------
Connecticut	51,500	102 85	5,296,775	------	-------	------
New York	652,800	102 49	66,905,472	19,300	$124 23	$2,397,639
New Jersey	115,800	130 00	15,054,000	14,800	140 00	2,072,000

ESTIMATED TOTAL NUMBER AND TOTAL VALUE OF EACH KIND OF LIVE
STOCK, AND THE AVERAGE PRICE IN FEBRUARY 1871.—Continued.

STATES.	HORSES.			MULES.		
	Number.	Average price.	Value.	Number.	Average price.	Value.
Pennsylvania	540,700	$106 92	$57,811,644	25,200	$132 51	$3,339,252
Delaware	20,000	89 99	1,799,800	4,000	130 99	523,900
Maryland	102,500	90 52	9,278,300	10,800	123 86	1,337,688
Virginia	178,500	84 93	15,100,005	29,400	108 93	3,302,542
North Carolina	126,700	90 41	11,454,947	44,400	114 43	5,080,692
South Carolina	53,800	101 97	5,485,986	42,300	108 25	4,578,975
Georgia	112,800	109 15	12,312,120	88,300	131 64	11,623,812
Florida	16,200	121 36	1,966,032	9,900	99 66	986,634
Alabama	103,000	99 34	10,291,624	98,700	116 93	11,540,991
Mississippi	82,000	104 22	8,608,572	96,300	127 74	12,301,362
Louisiana	70,800	91 29	6,463,332	75,500	134 79	10,176,645
Texas	615,700	32 29	19,840,953	82,900	52 30	4,335,670
Arkansas	138,100	73 98	10,216,638	67,900	93 51	6,349,329
Tennessee	280,000	84 48	23,654,400	94,600	105 51	9,981,246
West Virginia	97,800	81 83	8,002,974	2,300	92 08	211,784
Kentucky	327,400	75 05	24,571,370	85,500	82 73	7,073,415
Missouri	483,000	63 61	30,723,630	83,400	83 43	6,958,062
Illinois	1,008,800	70 26	70,878,288	96,900	85 18	8,253,942
Indiana	650,000	72 38	47,047,000	35,700	74 33	2,653,581
Ohio	724,200	79 48	57,559,416	22,200	83 36	1,850,592
Michigan	274,200	79 69	21,874,905	4,200	93 08	390,936
Wisconsin	310,200	79 87	24,775,674	4,800	106 55	511,440
Minnesota	119,900	79 13	9,487,687	2,700	104 15	281,205
Iowa	570,400	71 15	40,583,960	34,400	83 24	2,863,456
Kansas	156,000	72 15	11,255,400	14,900	92 14	1,372,886
Nebraska	36,200	83 05	3,006,410	3,400	119 35	405,790
California	204,800	50 26	10,293,248	21,400	65 64	1,404,696
Oregon	73,400	54 29	3,984,886	4,200	50 82	213,444
Nevada	8,600	58 66	504,476	1,000	75 00	75,000
The Territories	76,000	53 66	4,078,160	21,000	84 72	1,779,120
Total	8,702,000	....	$683,257,587	1,242,300	....	$126,127,786

STATES	OXEN AND OTHER CATTLE.			MILCH COWS.		
Maine	191,200	$36 98	$7,070,576	141,300	$36 37	$5,139,081
New Hampshire	133,000	36 62	4,870,460	95,000	37 50	3,562,500
Vermont	140,000	42 80	6,017,680	193,900	47 50	9,210,250
Massachusetts	122,700	44 66	5,479,782	139,300	59 16	8,240,988
Rhode Island	18,800	51 91	975,908	21,900	44 25	969,075
Connecticut	128,700	45 57	5,864,859	110,200	53 50	5,895,700
New York	705,000	42 27	29,800,350	1,411,100	48 51	68,452,461
New Jersey	84,100	45 00	3,789,546	145,000	61 38	8,900,100
Pennsylvania	760,900	41 41	31,508,869	788,900	46 67	36,817,963
Delaware	31,900	25 70	819,830	26,000	35 00	910,000
Maryland	125,700	27 21	3,420,297	96,000	39 09	3,752,640
Virginia	397,800	21 34	8,489,052	229,500	29 09	6,676,155
North Carolina	298,400	10 68	3,186,912	203,400	22 57	4,590,738
South Carolina	174,400	12 08	2,106,752	147,500	23 22	3,424,950
Georgia	409,500	10 80	4,422,600	252,500	21 61	5,456,525
Florida	412,000	8 17	3,366,040	73,500	15 83	1,163,505
Alabama	324,900	12 34	4,009,206	177,200	24 50	4,341,400
Mississippi	333,500	14 59	4,865,765	182,000	25 34	4,611,880
Louisiana	172,600	15 62	2,696,012	90,000	24 62	2,215,800
Texas	3,220,000	7 37	23,731,400	596,500	12 83	7,653,095
Arkansas	221,900	11 82	2,622,858	132,600	22 14	2,935,764
Tennessee	338,100	14 77	4,993,737	233,600	23 57	5,505,952
West Virginia	233,200	29 81	6,951,692	117,300	34 73	4,073,829
Kentucky	400,400	31 10	12,452,440	227,200	38 14	8,665,408
Missouri	731,100	24 46	17,882,706	371,200	31 92	11,848,704
Illinois	1,224,000	26 02	31,848,480	683,400	37 68	25,750,512
Indiana	750,000	26 16	19,620,000	435,500	38 50	16,766,750
Ohio	800,700	35 34	28,296,738	734,400	45 09	33,114,096
Michigan	450,000	31 65	14,242,500	333,900	41 15	13,739,985
Wisconsin	388,500	26 86	10,435,110	386,200	35 26	13,617,412
Minnesota	228,900	22 75	5,207,475	153,600	32 91	5,054,976
Iowa	814,900	24 05	19,597,345	465,300	34 31	15,964,443
Kansas	345,000	28 84	9,967,104	162,000	38 46	6,230,520
Nebraska	54,500	29 95	1,632,275	34,800	41 81	1,454,988
California	490,000	26 92	13,190,800	186,800	46 36	8,660,048
Oregon	102,000	21 69	2,212,380	62,400	32 25	2,012,400
Nevada	26,700	30 60	817,020	7,100	50 00	355,000
The Territories	426,000	26 94	11,476,440	175,000	36 82	6,443,500
Total	16,212,200	....	$369,940,056	10,023,000	....	$374,179,093

ESTIMATED TOTAL NUMBER AND TOTAL VALUE OF EACH KIND OF LIVE
STOCK, ETC.—Continued.

STATES.	SHEEP.			HOGS.		
	Number.	Average price.	Value.	Number.	Average price.	Value.
Maine	415,000	$2 73	$1,132,950	67,600	$ 9 87	$667,212
New Hampshire.	234,000	2 35	549,900	47,200	17 78	839,216
Vermont	548,000	2 62	1,435,760	66,700	17 00	1,133,900
Massachusetts ...	72,000	3 26	234,720	84,800	15 55	1,318,640
Rhode Island	30,000	3 71	111,300	20,400	14 62	298,248
Connecticut......	81,000	4 07	329,670	69,300	18 75	1,299,375
New York	2,080,000	3 14	6,531,200	658,800	11 09	7,306,092
New Jersey......	127,400	4 81	612,794	156,000	15 45	2,410,200
Pennsylvania	1,762,500	3 16	5,569,500	1,047,600	10 72	11,230,272
Delaware.........	25,300	3 75	94,875	46,000	6 25	287,500
Maryland	135,000	3 86	521,100	259,200	7 76	2,011,392
Virginia..........	394,800	2 37	935,676	757,500	5 60	4,242,000
North Carolina...	315,200	1 63	513,776	841,500	4 15	3,492,225
South Carolina....	156,700	1 95	305,565	317,200	4 69	1,487,668
Georgia	269,500	1 65	444,675	1,428,900	4 64	6,630,096
Florida	30,800	1 31	40,348	180,000	2 75	495,000
Alabama	200,200	1 77	354,354	900,000	4 30	3,870,000
Mississippi	200,000	2 00	400,000	850,000	4 40	3,740,000
Louisiana	90,000	2 18	196,200	300,000	4 30	1,290,000
Texas	1,137,300	1 40	1,592,220	1,200,000	2 76	3,312,000
Arkansas	135,000	2 32	313,200	863,800	3 28	2,832,608
Tennessee........	400,000	1 66	664,000	1,520,000	4 49	6,824,800
West Virginia ...	562,600	2 11	1,187,086	319,000	4 80	1,531,200
Kentucky	904,300	2 53	2,287,879	1,994,100	4 81	9,591,621
Missouri	1,578,200	1 61	2,540,902	2,200,000	4 34	9,548,000
Illinois...........	1,424,000	1 98	2,819,520	3,363,000	7 52	25,289,760
Indiana	2,100,000	1 82	3,822,000	2,349,000	6 04	14,187,960
Ohio	4,641,000	2 26	10,488,660	2,033,000	7 89	16,040,370
Michigan.........	3,072,800	2 23	6,852,344	517,400	7 37	3,813,238
Wisconsin	1,056,000	2 44	2,576,640	651,900	7 93	5,169,567
Minnesota	140,000	2 22	310,800	177,000	6 61	1,169,970
Iowa	1,822,700	1 71	3,116,817	3,100,000	7 15	22,165,000
Kansas	115,000	2 53	290,950	304,800	8 88	2,706,624
Nebraska	26,700	2 24	59,808	76,200	8 58	653,796
California	3,036,000	2 59	9,417,000	459,000	5 94	2,726,460
Oregon...........	419,200	1 90	796,480	149,500	2 51	375,245
Nevada	12,800	4 31	55,168	4,300	7 49	32,207
The Territories ..	1,500,000	3 02	4,530,000	77,000	7 57	582,890
Total.....	31,851,000	......	$74,035,837	29,457,500	......	$182,602,352

CENSUS OF 1870.

POPULATION OF THE UNITED STATES.—GENERAL NATIVITY AND FOREIGN PARENTAGE.

[From the Report of the Superintendent of the Census.]

STATES AND TERRITORIES.	1870.			1860.		
	Total population.	Native born.	Foreign born.	Total population.	Native born.	Foreign born.
Total U. States.....	38,555,983	32,989,437	5,566,546	31,443,321	27,304,624	4,138,697
Total States........	38,113,253	32,640,907	5,472,346	31,183,744	27,084,592	4,099,152
Alabama	996,992	987,030	9,962	964,201	951,849	12,352
Arkansas	484,471	479,445	5,026	435,450	431,850	3,600
California	560,247	350,416	209,831	379,994	233,466	146,528
Connecticut........	537,454	423,815	113,639	460,147	379,451	80,696
Delaware...........	125,015	115,879	9,136	112,216	103,051	9,165
Florida	187,748	182,781	4,967	140,424	137,115	3,309
Georgia.............	1,184,109	1,172,982	11,127	1,057,286	1,045,615	11,671
Illinois.............	2,539,891	2,024,693	515,198	1,711,951	1,387,308	324,643
Indiana	1,680,637	1,539,163	141,474	1,350,428	1,232,144	118,284
Iowa	1,191,792	987,735	204,057	674,913	568,836	106,077
Kansas	364,399	316,007	48,392	107,206	94,515	12,691
Kentucky	1,321,011	1,257,613	63,398	1,155,684	1,095,885	59,799
Louisiana	726,915	665,088	61,827	708,002	627,027	80,975
Maine	626,915	578,034	48,881	628,279	590,826	37,453
Maryland	780,894	697,482	83,412	687,049	609,520	77,529
Massachusetts.....	1,457,351	1,104,032	353,319	1,231,066	970,960	260,106
Michigan...........	1,184,059	916,049	268,010	749,113	600,020	149,093
Minnesota	439,706	279,009	160,697	172,023	113,295	58,728
Mississippi........	827,922	816,731	11,191	791,305	782,747	8,558
Missouri	1,721,295	1,499,028	222,267	1,182,012	1,021,471	160,541
Nebraska..........	122,993	92,245	30,748	28,841	22,490	6,351
Nevada	42,491	23,690	18,801	6,857	4,793	2,064
New Hampshire....	318,300	288,689	29,611	326,073	305,135	20,938
New Jersey........	906,096	717,153	188,943	672,035	549,245	122,790
New York.........	4,382,759	3,244,406	1,138,353	3,880,735	2,879,455	1,001,280
North Carolina.....	1,071,361	1,068,332	3,029	992,622	989,324	3,298
Ohio...............	2,665,260	2,292,767	372,493	2,339,511	2,011,262	328,249
Oregon.............	90,923	79,323	11,600	52,465	47,342	5,123
Pennsylvania	3,521,791	2,976,530	545,261	2,906,215	2,475,710	430,505
Rhode Island	217,353	161,957	55,396	174,620	137,226	37,394
South Carolina.....	705,606	697,532	8,074	703,708	693,722	9,986
Tennessee..........	1,258,520	1,239,204	19,316	1,109,801	1,088,575	21,226
Texas	818,579	756,168	62,411	604,215	560,743	43,422
Vermont	330,551	283,396	47,155	315,098	282,355	32,743
Virginia...........	1,225,163	1,211,409	13,754	1,219,630	1,201,117	18,513
West Virginia	442,014	424,923	17,091	376,688	360,143	16,545
Wisconsin	1,054,670	690,171	364,499	775,881	498,954	276,927
Total Territories...	442,730	348,530	94,200	259,757	220,032	39,545
Arizona............	9,658	3,849	5,809	....	....	....
Colorado	39,864	33,265	6,599	34,277	31,611	2,666
Dakota.............	14,181	9,366	4,815	4,837	3,063	1,774
Dist. of Columbia..	131,700	115,446	16,254	75,080	62,596	12,484
Idaho	14,999	7,114	7,885	....	....	....
Montana............	20,595	12,616	7,979	....	....	....
New-Mexico	91,874	86,254	5,620	93,516	86,793	6,723
Utah	86,786	56,084	30,702	40,273	27,519	12,754
Washington	23,955	18,931	5,024	11,594	8,450	3,144
Wyoming..........	9,118	5,605	3,513	....	....	....

POPULATION OF ALL THE CITIES OF THE UNITED STATES.

[This table has been carefully compiled from the census (official copy) of 1870. It embraces all the cities returned as such, with a few that appear to have been omitted as cities distinctively.]

STATES AND CITIES.	Total Population.	STATES AND CITIES.	Total Population.	STATES AND CITIES.	Total Population.
Alabama.		*Illinois.—contd.*		*Iowa—continued.*	
Eufaula	3,185	Decatur	7,161	Independence	2,945
Huntsville	4,907	Dixon	4,055	Iowa City	5,914
Mobile	32,034	Elgin	5,441	Keokuk	12,766
Montgomery	10,588	El Paso	1,564	Lyons	4,088
Selma	6,484	Freeport	7,889	Maquoketa	1,756
Talladega	1,933	Galena	7,019	Marshalltown	3,218
Tuscaloosa	1,689	Galesburg	10,158	McGregor	2,074
Tuscumbia	1,214	Jacksonville	9,203	Muscatine	6,718
Total	62,034	Joliet	7,263	Oskaloosa	3,204
Arkansas.		La Salle	5,200	Ottumwa	5,214
Little Rock	12,380	Litchfield	3,852	Sioux City	3,401
California.		Macomb	2,748	Waterloo	4,337
Los Angeles	5,728	Mendota	3,546	Waverley	2,291
Marysville	4,738	Monmouth	4,662	Winterset	1,485
Oakland	10,500	Morris	3,138	Total	160,630
Sacramento	16,283	Mound City	1,631	**Kansas.**	
San Diego	2,300	Mt. Carmel	1,640	Atchison	7,054
San Francisco	149,473	Olney	2,680	Baxter Springs	1,284
San Jose	9,089	Ottawa	7,736	Emporia	2,168
Stockton	10,066	Pekin	5,696	Fort Scott	4,147
Total	208,177	Peoria	22,849	Lawrence	8,320
Connecticut.		Peru	3,650	Leavenworth	17,873
Bridgeport	18,969	Quincy	24,052	Ottawa	2,941
Hartford	37,180	Rockford	11,049	Paola	1,811
Middletown	6,923	Rock Island	7,890	Topeka	5,790
New Haven	50,840	Shelbyville	2,051	Wyandotte	2,940
Norwich	16,653	Springfield	17,364	Total	54,355
Waterbury	10,826	Sterling	3,998	**Kentucky.**	
Total	141,391	Watseca	1,551	Covington	24,505
Colorado.		Waukegan	4,507	Frankfort	5,336
Denver	4,759	Total	571,021	Henderson	4,171
Delaware.		**Indiana.**		Hopkinsville	3,136
Wilmington	30,841	Columbia	1,663	Lexington	14,801
Dist. of Columbia.		Connorsville	2,496	Louisville	100,753
Georgetown	11,384	Crawfordsville	3,701	Maysville	4,705
Washington	109,199	Evansville	21,830	Newport	15,087
Total	120,583	Fort Wayne	17,718	Owensboro	3,437
Florida.		Franklin City	2,707	Paducah	6,866
Jacksonville	6,912	Goshen	3,133	Paris	2,655
Pensacola	3,347	Greencastle	3,227	Total	185,512
St. Augustine	1,717	Indianapolis	48,244	**Louisiana.**	
Tallahassee	2,023	Jeffersonville	7,254	Baton Rouge	6,498
Total	13,999	Kendallville	2,164	Donaldsonville	1,573
Georgia.		Lafayette	13,506	New Orleans	191,418
Athens	4,251	Laporte	6,581	Shreveport	4,607
Atlanta	21,789	Lawrenceburg	3,139	Total	204,096
Augusta	15,389	Logansport	8,950	**Maine.**	
Columbus	7,401	Madison	10,709	Auburn	6,169
Macon	10,810	Michigan City	3,985	Augusta	7,808
Milledgeville	2,750	New Orleans	15,396	Bangor	18,289
Rome	2,748	Peru	3,617	Bath	7,371
Savannah	28,235	Richmond	9,445	Belfast	5,278
Total	93,373	Seymour	2,372	Biddeford	10,282
Idaho.		Shelbyville	2,731	Calais	5,944
Boise City	995	South Bend	7,206	Hallowell	3,007
Idaho City	889	Terre Haute	16,103	Lewiston	13,600
Silver City	599	Valparaiso	2,765	Portland	31,413
Total	2,483	Vincennes	5,440	Rockland	7,074
Illinois.		Wabash City	2,881	Total	116,235
Alton	8,665	Total	228,983	**Maryland.**	
Amboy	2,825	**Iowa.**		Annapolis	5,744
Anna	1,269	Burlington	14,930	Baltimore	267,354
Aurora	11,162	Cedar Falls	3,070	Frederick	8,526
Belleville	8,146	Cedar Rapids	5,940	Hagerstown	5,779
Bloomington	14,590	Clinton	6,129	Total	287,403
Bushnell	2,003	Council Bluffs	10,020	**Massachusetts.**	
Cairo	6,267	Davenport	20,038	Boston	250,526
Canton	3,308	Des Moines	12,035	Cambridge	39,634
Centralia	3,190	Dubuque	18,434	Charlestown	28,323
Champaign	4,625	Fairfield	2,226	Chelsea	18,547
Chicago	298,977	Fort Dodge	3,095	Fall River	26,766
Danville	4,751	Fort Madison	4,011	Haverhill	13,092
		Glenwood	1,291		

POPULATION OF ALL THE CITIES OF THE UNITED STATES.—Continued.

States and Cities.	Total Population.	States and Cities.	Total Population.	States and Cities.	Total Population.
Mass.—continued.		*Missouri—cont'd.*		*Ohio.*	
Lawrence	28,921	St. Louis	310,864	Akron	10,006
Lowell	40,928	Westport	1,095	Canton	8,660
Lynn	28,233			Chillicothe	8,920
New Bedford	21,320	Total	401,963	Cincinnati	216,239
Newburyport	12,595	*Montana.*		Circleville	5,407
Salem	24,117	Helena	3,842	Cleveland	92,829
Springfield	26,703	*Nebraska.*		Columbus	31,274
Taunton	18,629	Omaha	16,083	Dayton	30,473
Worcester	41,105	Nebraska City	6,050	Fremont	5,455
				Galliopolis	3,711
Total	619,439	Total	22,133	Hamilton	11,081
Michigan.		*Nevada.*		Ironton	5,686
Adrian	8,438	Austin	1,324	Lancaster	4,725
Ann Arbor	7,363	Carson City	3,042	Mansfield	8,029
Battle Creek	5,838	Virginia	7,048	Marietta	5,218
Bay City	7,064			Massillon	5,185
Big Rapids	1,227	Total	11,414	Mt. Vernon	4,876
Coldwater	4,381	*New Hampshire.*		Newark	6,698
Corunna	1,408	Concord	12,241	Piqua	5,927
Detroit	79,577	Dover	9,294	Pomeroy	5,824
East Saginaw	11,350	Manchester	23,536	Portsmouth	10,592
Flint	5,386	Nashua	10,543	Sandusky	13,000
Grand Haven	3,147	Portsmouth	9,211	Springfield	12,652
Grand Rapids	16'507			Steubenville	8,107
Hillsdale	3,518	Total	64,825	Tiffin	5,648
Holland	2,319	*New Jersey.*		Toledo	31,584
Jackson	11,447	Atlantic City	1,043	Urbana	4,276
Lansing	5,241	Brighton	6,830	Warren	3,457
Lapeer	1,772	Burlington	5,817	Wooster	5,419
Manistee	3,343	Camden	20,045	Xenia	6,377
Marshall	4,925	Elizabeth	20,832	Youngstown	8,075
Monroe	5,986	Harrison	4,129	Zanesville	10,011
Muskegon	6,002	Hoboken	20,297		
Niles	4,630	Jersey City	82,546	Total	595,461
Owasso	2,065	Millville	6,101	*Oregon.*	
Pontiac	4,867	Newark	105,059	Oregon City	1,382
Port Huron	5,973	New Brunswick	15,058	Portland	8,293
Saginaw	7,460	Orange	9,348		
St. Clair	1,790	Paterson	33,579	Total	9,675
Wyandotte	2,731	Plainfield	5,095	*Pennsylvania.*	
Ypsilanti	5,471	Princeton	2,798	Allegheny	53,180
		Rahway	6,258	Allentown	13,884
Total	229,336	Trenton	22,874	Altoona	10,610
Minnesota.				Carbondale	6,393
Duluth	3,131	Total	367,709	Chester	9,485
Hastings	3,458	*New Mexico.*		Columbia	6,461
Mankato	3,482	Santa Fe	4,765	Corry	6,809
Minneapolis	13,066	*New York.*		Erie	19,646
Owatonna	2,070	Albany	69,422	Harrisburg	23,103
Red Wing	4,260	Auburn	17,225	Lancaster	20,233
Rochester	3,953	Binghamton	12,692	Lock Haven	6,989
St. Anthony	5,013	Brooklyn	396,099	Meadville	7,103
St. Cloud	2,161	Buffalo	117,714	Philadelphia	674,022
St. Paul	20,030	Cohoes	15,357	Pittsburgh	86,076
Winona	7,192	Elmira	15,863	Reading	33,930
		Hudson	8,615	Scranton	35,092
Total	67,816	Lockport	12,426	Titusville	8,639
Mississippi.		Newburg	17,014	Williamsport	16,030
Columbus	4,812	New York	942,292	York	11,003
Grenada	1,887	Ogdensburg	10,076		
Holly Springs	2,406	Oswego	20,910	Total	1,048,686
Jackson	4,234	Poughkeepsie	20,080	*Rhode Island.*	
Macon	975	Rochester	62,386	Newport	12,521
Natchez	9,057	Rome	11,000	Providence	68,904
Vicksburgh	12,443	Schenectady	11,026		
		Syracuse	43,051	Total	81,425
Total	35,814	Troy	46,465	*South Carolina.*	
Missouri.		Utica	28,804	Charleston	48,956
Cape Girardeau	3,585	Watertown	9,336	Columbia	9,298
Chillicothe	3,978				
Hannibal	10,125	Total	1,887,853	Total	58,254
Independence	3,184	*North Carolina.*		*Tennessee.*	
Jefferson City	4,420	Charlotte	4,473	Chattanooga	6,093
Kansas City	32,260	Fayetteville	4,660	Knoxville	8,682
Louisiana	3,639	Newberne	5,849	Memphis	40,226
Macon	3,678	Raleigh	7,790	Nashville	25,865
St. Charles	5,570	Wilmington	13,446		
St. Joseph	19,565			Total	80,866
		Total	36,218		

POPULATION OF ALL THE CITIES OF THE UNITED STATES.—Continued.

States and Cities.	Total Population.	States and Cities.	Total Population.	States and Cities.	Total Population.
Texas.		*Vermont.—cont'd.*		*Wisconsin.*	
Austin.........	4,428	Montpelier.....	3,023	Appleton	4,518
Browneville....	4,905	Rutland....... .	9,834	Beaver Dam....	3,265
Galveston......	13,818	St. Albans.....	7,014	Beloit.........	4,396
Houston.......	9,382	St. Johnsbury..	4,665	Fond du Lac...	12,764
San Antonio ...	12,256	Total...........	49,443	Green Bay.....	4,666
Total...........	44,789	*Virginia.*		Janesville......	8,789
Utah.		Alexandria	13,570	Kenosha.......	4,309
Logan	1,757	Fredericksb'gh	4,046	La Crosse.....'	7,785
Manti..........	1,239	Lynchburgh....	6,825	Madison........	9,176
Mt. Pleasant...	1,346	Norfolk.........	19,229	Manitowoc.....	5,168
Ogden	3,127	Petersburgh ...	18,950	Milwaukee.....	71,440
Salt Lake City.	12,854	Portsmouth.....	10,492	Oshkosh	12,663
Total..........	20,323	Richmond......	51,038	Portage.........	3,945
Vermont.		Total...........	124,150	Racine.........	9,880
Bennington	2,501	*West Virginia.*		Sheboygan	5,310
Brattleboro	4,933	Parkersburg ...	5,546	Watertown....	7,550
Burlington.....	14,387	Wheeling	19,280		
Middlebury	3,086	Total..........	24,826	Total............	175,624

ORDER OF THE STATES IN POINT OF POPULATION, AT SEVERAL PERIODS.

	1790.	1830.	1850.	1860.	1870.
1	Virginia.........	New York	New York	New York......	New York.......
2	Massachusetts ...	Pennsylvania ...	Pennsylvania ...	Pennsylvania...	Pennsylvania ....
3	Pennsylvania....	Virginia	Ohio	Ohio	Ohio ....
4	North Carolina..	Ohio	Virginia	Illinois.........	Illinois...........
5	New York	North Carolina..	Tennessee.......	Virginia.........	Missouri.........
6	Maryland	Kentucky........	Massachusetts ..	Indiana.........	Indiana..........
7	South Carolina...	Tennessee	Indiana.........	Massachusetts...	Massachusetts ...
8	Connecticut......	Massachusetts ...	Kentucky	Missouri........	Kentucky.......
9	New Jersey	South Carolina...	Georgia.........	Tennessee......	Tennessee ....
10	New Hampshire .	Georgia..........	North Carolina .	Kentucky'......	Virginia ....
11	Vermont.........	Maryland	Illinois.........	Georgia.........	Iowa............
12	Georgia.........	Maine	Alabama........	North Carolina..	Georgia.........
13	Kentucky	Indiana	Missouri........	Alabama........	Michigan ....
14	Rhode Island .	New Jersey	South Carolina..	Mississippi......	North Carolina...
15	Delaware........	Alabama	Mississippi	Wisconsin.......	Wisconsin ....
16	Tennessee	Connecticut	Maine	Michigan	Alabama........
17		Vermont.........	Maryland	Maryland	New Jersey......
18		New Hampshire .	Louisiana........	South Carolina..	Mississippi ....
19		Louisiana	New Jersey	Iowa............	Texas............
20		Illinois	Michigan.	New Jersey	Maryland........
21		Missouri........	Connecticut.....	Louisiana	Louisiana........
22		Mississippi......	New Hampshire..	Maine...........	South Carolina...
23		Rhode Island....	Vermont........	Texas...........	Maine ....
24		Delaware........	Wisconsin :.....	Connecticut.....	California.........
25		Florida	Texas...........	Arkansas	Connecticut......
26		Michigan	Arkansas	California........	Arkansas ....
27		Arkansas	Iowa	New Hampshire..	West Virginia....
28			Rhode Island.....	Vermont........	Kansas ....
29			California........	Rhode Island	Minnesota ....
30			Delaware	Minnesota	Vermont.........
31			Florida	Florida	New Hampshire .
32			Minnesota	Kansas	Rhode Island . ...
33				Delaware	Florida ....
34				Oregon	Delaware ....
35					Nebraska ....
36					Oregon ....
37					Nevada ....

ORDER OF TERRITORIES, 1870.

District of Columbia, New Mexico, Utah, Colorado, Washington, Montana, Idaho, Dacotah, Arizona, Wyoming. The census of Alaska has not been taken.

POPULATION OF STATES BY RACES.

	Whites.	Colored.	Indians.	Chinese.
Alabama	531,384	475,510	98	
Arizona	9,581	26	31	20
Arkansas	362,115	122,169	89	98
*California	499,424	4,272	7,241	49,310
Colorado	39,221	456	180	7
Connecticut	527,449	9,668	239	2²
Dakota	12,887	94	1,200	
Delaware	10,224	22,994		
District of Columbia	88,278	45,405	15	3
Florida	96,057	91,689	2	
Georgia	638,926	545,142	4	1
Idaho	10,618	60	47	4,274
Illinois	2,511,096	28,762	32	1
Indiana	1,655,837	24,560	240	
Iowa	1,185,979	5,762	48	
Kansas	346,377	17,108	914	
Kentucky	1,098,692	222,210	108	1
Louisiana	362,065	364,210	569	713
Maine	62,480	1,600	499	1
Maryland	605,497	195,391	4	2
*Massachusetts	1,443,156	13,947	151	97
Michigan	1,168,282	11,849	4,926	2
Minnesota	438,257	759	690	
Mississippi	382,896	444,201	809	16
Missouri	1,603,146	118,071	75	32
Montana	18,306	183	157	1,949
Nebraska	122,117	789	87	
Nevada	38,959	357	23	3,152
New Hampshire	317,697	580	23	
*New Jersey	875,407	30,658	16	15
New Mexico	90,393	172	1,309	
New York	4,330,210	52,081	439	29
North Carolina	678,740	391,650	1,241	
Ohio	2,601,446	63,213	100	1
Oregon	86,829	346	318	3,330
Pennsylvania	3,456,449	65,294	34	14
Rhode Island	212,219	4,980	154	
South Carolina	289,669	415,814	124	1
Tennessee	936,119	322,331	70	
Texas	564,700	253,475	379	25
Utah	86,048	114	175	449
Vermont	329,613	924	14	
Virginia	712,089	512,841	229	4
Washington Territory	22,195	207	1,319	234
West Virginia		19,980	1	
Wisconsin	1,051,351	2,113	1,206	
Wyoming	8,726	183	66	143

* Japanese:—California, 33; Massachusetts, 10; New Jersey 10.

COMPARATIVE INCREASE OF POPULATION.

Census.	Population.	Increase, Per Cent.
1790	3,929,827	....
1800	5,305,937	35.09
1810	7,239,814	36.45
1820	9,638,191	33.13
1830	12,866,020	33.49
1840	17,069,453	32.67
1850	23,191,876	35.87
1860	31,445,080	35.58
1870	38,549,987	22.59

AREA OF THE UNITED STATES.

	Acres.
Total area of the public lands of the States and Territories	1,400,549,033
Total area of those States where there are no public lands	476,546,560
Area of Indian Territory	44,154,240
Area of District of Columbia	38,400
Grand total of area of the United States, in acres	1,921,288,233

Or *three millions two thousand and thirteen square miles.*

This does not include the area of the great lakes just within and forming a portion of our Northern boundary; neither does it include the marine league on the coast.

RAILROADS OF THE UNITED STATES.

IN 1851 there were 8,876 miles of railroad in operation in this country, and the total earnings in that year amounted to $39,466,358; in 1870, over 50,000 miles were in operation, and at $9.000 per mile. the earnings amounted to $450,000,000; the increase per year between 1851 and 1870 thus being shown to equal the enormous sum of $20,000,000.

The tonnage transported by the railroads in 1851 equaled 5,000,000. In 1870, the net tonnage equaled 72,500.000 tons; the increase of tonnage in a period of twenty years equaled 67,500.000, or at the rate of 3,375,000 yearly. The value of the railroad tonnage transported in 1851, at $150 per ton, equaled $810,725,200. In 1870, its value, at $150 per ton, equaled $10,875,750,000. The total increase of value in this period of twenty years equaled $10,065,354,800. The annual increase of value equaled $503,267,740.

PROGRESS OF RAILROADS IN THE UNITED STATES—A TABULAR STATEMENT OF THE MILEAGE OF RAILROADS IN EACH STATE AND GROUP OF STATES, AT THE END OF THE SEVERAL YEARS GIVEN BELOW.

STATES.	1841.	1850.	1855.	1860.	1865.	1866.	1867.	1868.	1869.	1870.
Maine	11	245	415	472	521	521	521	560	680	786
New Hampshire	53	467	657	661	667	667	667	667	702	736
Vermont	....	290	529	554	587	587	587	605	614	614
Massachusetts	373	1035	1264	1264	1297	1331	1401	*1425	1460	1460
Rhode Island	50	68	108	108	125	125	125	125	125	136
Connecticut	102	402	496	601	637	637	637	637	692	742
New Eng'd States.	589	2508	3469	3660	3834	3868	3938	4019	4293	4494
New York	538	1361	2583	2682	3002	3178	3245	3329	3658	3928
New Jersey	196	206	466	560	864	879	942	973	1011	1125
Pennsylvania	754	1240	1800	2598	3728	4091	4311	4398	4598	4656
Delaware	39	39	56	127	134	147	165	165	210	224
Maryland & D. C.	259	259	327	386	446	484	527	535	588	671
West Virginia	61	97	241	352	365	365	365	365	387	387
Middle States,	1837	3202	5473	6706	8539	9144	9555	9765	10,452	10,991
Ohio	36	575	1486	2946	3331	3372	3398	3398	3448	3538
Michigan	138	342	474	779	941	1039	1163	1199	1325	1638
Indiana	....	228	1406	2163	3217	2217	2506	2600	2852	3177
Illinois	22	111	887	2790	3157	3191	3224	3440	4031	4823
Wisconsin	....	20	187	905	1010	1036	1036	1235	1512	1525
Minnesota	....	....	....	....	213	298	482	572	795	1072
Iowa	....	....	68	655	891	908	1283	1523	2095	2683
Kansas	....	....	....	....	40	240	494	648	931	1501
Nebraska, etc	....	....	....	....	122	305	555	920	1058	1812
Missouri	....	....	139	817	925	925	1085	1354	1712	2000
Western States.	196	1276	4567	11,064	12,847	13,621	15,226	16,889	19,765	23,769
Virginia	223	384	912	1379	1401	1442	1464	1464	1483	1486
North Carolina	87	283	582	937	984	1042	1042	1097	1130	1178
South Carolina	204	289	759	973	1007	1007	1007	1076	1101	1139
Georgia	271	643	1020	1420	1420	1502	1548	1575	1652	1845
Florida	....	21	21	402	416	416	437	437	446	446
Alabama	46	183	334	743	805	839	851	953	1091	1429
Mississippi	14	75	278	862	898	898	892	898	990	990
Louisiana	40	80	203	335	335	335	335	335	375	479
Texas	....	....	40	307	465	471	513	513	583	711
Kentucky	28	78	242	534	567	581	635	813	852	1017
Tennessee	....	....	466	1253	1296	1296	1359	1436	1451	1492
Arkansas	....	....	....	38	38	38	38	86	128	256
Southern States.	913	2035	4857	9182	9632	9867	10,126	10,693	11,272	12,468
California	....	....	8	23	214	308	382	466	702	925
Oregon	....	....	....	....	19	19	19	19	60	159
Nevada	....	....	....	....	....	....	30	402	402	593
Pacific States.	....	....	8	23	233	327	431	889	1164	1677

RECAPITULATION.

STATES.	1841.	1850.	1855.	1860.	1865.	1866.	1867.	1868.	1869.	1870.
New Eng. States.	589	2,508	3,469	3,660	3,834	3,868	3,938	4,019	4,301	4,494
Middle States	1,837	3,202	5,473	6,706	8,539	9,144	9,555	9,765	10,752	10,991
Western States	196	1,276	4,567	11,064	12,847	16,621	15,226	16,889	19,765	23,769
Southern States	913	2,035	4,857	9,182	9,632	6,867	10,126	10,683	11,272	12,468
Pacific States	....	....	8	23	233	327	431	889	1,164	1,677
Grand Total	3,535	9,021	18,374	30,635	35,085	36,827	39,276	42,255	47,254	53,399

RATES OF POSTAGE

BETWEEN THE UNITED STATES AND GREAT BRITAIN AND OTHER FOREIGN
COUNTRIES.

The standard single rate to Great Britain is ½ oz. avoirdupois; to France and the Continent (by French mails), it is 15 grammes, or ¼ oz. avoirdupois.

The asterisk (*) indicates that prepayment of the rate to which it is affixed is optional; in all other cases prepayment is required.

DESTINATION.	Letters not exceeding ¼ oz.	Letters not exceeding ½ oz.	News-papers.
	cts.	cts.	cts.
England, Ireland, Scotland, and Wales......................		*6	2
Books, pamphlets, circulars, and other printed matter, per single rate of 4 oz., 6 cents.			
Samples of merchandise, seeds, etc., per single rate of 4 oz., 8 cents. No packet is allowed to exceed 24 inches in length by 12 inches in breadth and 12 inches in thickness. These rates must be *fully prepaid in stamps*, or the package will not be forwarded. Letters and packets may be registered at an extra fee of 8 cents—to be prepaid.			
German states and free cities, including Austria, Bavaria, Baden, Bremen, Brunswick, Frankfort, Hamburg, Hanover, Luxemburg, Lubec, Mecklenburg, Oldenburg, Prussia, Saxe-Altenburg, Coburg-Gotha, Meiningen, Weimar, Saxony, and Wurtemburg, by North German Union......		*7	3
" " " closed mail, *via* England............		*10	4
Australia, British mail, *via* Southampton....................		16	6
" " *via* Marseilles....................		24	8
Azores, French mail.....................................			
" ship mail..		5	2
" *via* England and France..........................	16	28	8
" *via* Southampton................................		16	6
Bahama Islands, by steamer from New York...............		3	2
Belgium...		*10	4
China, American Packet, *via* San Francisco		10	2
" *via* North German Union, direct....................		24	12
" " " closed mail, *via* England....		27	13
" French mail......................................			
" British mail, *via* Southampton		28	6
" " *via* Marseilles.....................		36	8
Constantinople, *via* North German Union direct.............		*12	
" " " closed mail, *via* Eng.		*15	8
" *via* England	16	28	6
" French mail...................................			
Cuba..		10	2
East Indies, British mail, *via* Southampton...............		22	6
" " *via* Marseilles....................		30	8
" *via* North German Union direct..............		24	12
" " " " closed mail, *via* Eng'd.		27	13
" *via* San Francisco..........................		*10	2
Egypt (except Alexandria), *via* North German Union, direct		*17	9
" " " " " *via* England..		*20	10
Egypt (except Alexandria), British mail, *via* Southampton.		16	4
" " " " *via* Marseilles....	16	28	6
" (to Alexandria), *via* Nor. Ger. Un. direct.............		*12	8
" " " closed mail, *via* Eng.		*15	9
" " by British mail, *via* Southampton...		16	4
" " " " *via* Marseilles......	16	28	6
" " by French mail.....................			

RATES OF POSTAGE.—Continued.

The asterisk (*) indicates that prepayment of the rate to which it is affixed is optional; in all other cases prepayment is required.

DESTINATION.	Letters not exceeding ¼ oz.	Letters not exceeding ½ oz.	News-papers.
	cts.	cts.	cts.
France		*10	2
Greece, *via* North German Un. direct..................		*15	9
" " closed mail, *via* England.....		*18	10
" (newspapers under 2 oz., 7 cts. each, by direct mail, and 8 cts. each by closed mail, *via* England.)			
Greece, French mail...................................			
Holland....		*10	4
Italy, direct closed mail		*10	4
" *via* North German Union direct..................		.11	7
" " closed mail, *via* England.....		14	8
" French mail....................................			
Japan, British mail, *via* Southampton...............		28	
" " " Marseilles..............		36	8
" *via* North German Union direct.................		24	12
" " closed mail, *via* England....		27	13
" French mail, *via* Yokahama....................			
" (to Yokahama) by French mail...................			
" American packet, *via* San Francisco		10	2
Java, British mail, *via* Southampton...............		28	6
" " " Marseilles..............		36	8
" French mail....................................			
Jerusalem, *via* North German Union direct...........		*12	7
" " closed mail, *via* England		*15	8
" French mail.............................			
Mexico		10	3
Naples and Sardinian States, direct closed mail, *via* England		*10	4
" " *via* North German Union direct..		*11	7
" " " " closed mail, *via* England..............................		*14	8
Naples and Sardinian States, French mail			
Portugal, French mail................................			
" *via* England..............................	16	28	8
Roman or Papal States, *via* Nor. Ger. Un. direct............		*11	6
" " " closed mail, *via* Eng.		*14	7
" " " French mail.........			
Russia, *via* Nor. Ger. Un. direct (if prepaid, 12 cents).......		*15	5
" " " clos'd mail, *via* Eng. (if prep'd, 15 c.)		*18	6
Sandwich Islands, by mail from San Francisco		6	2
South American States, *Atlantic Coast*, *via* England........		28	4
" " for Brazil alone, from New York....		*15	2
" " *Pacific Coast*, Peru, Ecuador, Bolivia, and Chili..		22	4
South American States, Argentine Republic, Buenos Ayres, Montevideo, from New York...........................		18	4
Spain, French mail...................................			
" *via* England..............................	16	28	6
Sweden, *via* N. Ger. Un. direct (if prepaid, 11 cents)........		*13	8
" " clos'd mail, *via* Eng. (if prep'd, 14 cts.)		*16	9
" (newspapers under 2 oz., 6 cents each by direct mail, and 7 cents each by closed mail, *via* England.)			
Switzerland, direct closed mail, *via* England..............		*15	11
" French mail.............................			
" *via* North German Union direct.............		*12	10
" closed mail............................		*10	4
West Indies (British and Danish), American packet 23d of each month, from New York...........................		10	2
West Indies (British), British mail, *via* St. Thomas......		10	2
" (not British), " "		18	4

RATES OF DOMESTIC POSTAGE.

LETTERS.

The standard single rate weight is ½ oz. avoirdupois.

Single rate letter, throughout the United States................................ 3 cts.
For each additional ½ oz. or fraction... 3 "
Drop letters, for local delivery, single rate.................................... 2 "
Drop letters, where there is no local delivery, single rate..................... 1 "
Advertised letters are charged extra.. 1 "

These postages must be prepaid by stamps. Letters are to be forwarded without additional charge, if the person to whom they are addressed has changed his residence, and has left proper directions to such effect. Letters uncalled for will be returned to the sender, if a request to that effect be written upon the envelope. Properly certified letters of soldiers and sailors will be forwarded without prepayment. No extra charge is made for the service of carriers taking letters to or from post-offices.

NEWSPAPERS.

The standard single rate is 4 oz. avoirdupois.

Daily (seven times a week).. 35 cts. per quarter.
Daily (six times a week)... 30 "   "
Tri-weekly .... 15 "   "
Semi-weekly .... 10 "   "
Weekly .... 5 "   "

These rates must be prepaid quarterly or yearly; for full security they should be prepaid at the office where the paper is received. One copy of a weekly newspaper may be sent free by the publisher to each subscriber who resides in the county where the paper is published.

PERIODICALS

The standard single rate is 4 oz. avoirdupois.

Semi-monthly .... 6 cts. per quarter.
Monthly .... 3 "   "
Quarterly .... 1 "   "

TRANSIENT PRINTED MATTER.

Books, for each single rate of 4 oz. avoirdupois................................ 4 cts.
Circulars, not exceeding three in one envelope constituting a single rate.... 2 "
Miscellaneous mailable matter (embracing all pamphlets, occasional publications, transient newspapers, book manuscripts, and proof sheets, whether corrected or not, maps, prints, engravings, sheet music, blanks, flexible patterns, samples and sample cards, photographic paper, letter envelopes, postal envelopes or wrappers, cards, paper, plain or ornamental, photographic representations of different types, seeds, cuttings, bulbs, roots, and scions), in one package to one address, for each single rate of 4 oz. avoirdupois .... 2 "

[By a decision of the post-office department, manuscripts and proofs passing between authors and editors of magazines and newspapers, are not regarded as passing "between authors and publishers," and must pay letter postage.]

Prepayment by stamps is required for all postage on transient printed matter.

The maximum weight of any package of printed or miscellaneous matter is 4 lbs. avoirdupois.

Registration.—Letters may be registered on payment of a fee of twenty cents, but the Government takes no responsibilit for safe carriage or compensation in case of loss.

Money Orders.—All principal post-offices now receive small sums of money, and issue drafts for the same upon other post-offices, subject to the following charges and regulations :

On orders not exceeding $20... 10 cts.
Over $20 and not exceeding $30... 15 "
Over $30 and not exceeding $40... 20 "
Over $40 and not exceeding $50... 25 "

No fractions of cents to be introduced in an order. United States treasury notes or national bank notes only received or paid.

The order is only payable at the office upon which it is drawn. The order should be collected within one year from its date. After once paying an order, by whomsoever presented, the department will be liabla to no further claim.

RATES OF POSTAGE BETWEEN THE UNITED STATES AND BRITISH NORTH AMERICA.

LETTERS.

The standard single rate is $\frac{1}{2}$ oz. avoirdupois.

To or from the Dominion of Canada, irrespective of distance, if prepaid, 6 cents; otherwise... 10 cts.
To or from other British North American Provinces, for a distance of not over 3,000 miles... 10 "
For any distance over 3,000 miles... 15 "

Prepayment is optional, except to Newfoundland, to which prepayment is compulsory.

PRINTED MATTER.

The regular United States rates must be prepaid, but these only pay for transportation to the boundary line; a second fee is charged on delivery by the Provincial post-office.

HOMESTEAD FOR SOLDIERS.

THE LAW, THE INSTRUCTIONS, AND THE BLANK FOR APPLICATIONS.

DEPARTMENT OF THE INTERIOR,
GENERAL LAND OFFICE, Aug. 8, 1870.

GENTLEMEN:—The following is the twenty-fifth section of the act of Congress, approved July 15, 1870, entitled "An act making appropriations for the support of the army for the year ending June 30, 1871, and for other purposes," viz.:

SEC. 25.—*And be it further enacted*, That every private soldier and officer who has served in the army of the United States during the rebellion, for ninety days, and remained loyal to the Government, and every seaman, marine, and officer or other person who has served in the navy of the United States, or in the marine corps or revenue marine during the rebellion, for ninety days, and remained loyal to the Government, shall, on payment of the fee or commission to any Register or Receiver of any Land Office required by law, be entitled to enter one quarter section of land, not mineral, of the alternate reserved sections of public lands along the lines of any railroads or other public works in the United States, wherever public lands have been or may be granted by acts of Congress, and to receive a patent therefor under and by virtue of the provisions of the act to secure homesteads to actual settlers on the public domain, and the acts amendatory thereof, and on the terms and conditions therein prescribed; and all the provisions of said acts, except as herein modified, shall extend and be applicable to entries under this act, and the Commissioner of the General Land Office is hereby authorized to prescribe the necessary rules and regulations to carry this section into effect, and determine all facts necessary thereto.

By these provisions the Homestead Law of 20th May, 1862, and the acts amendatory thereof, are so modified as to allow entries to be made by the parties mentioned therein, of the maximum quantity of one quarter-section, or 160 acres of land, held at the double minimum price of $2.50 per acre, instead of one-half quarter-section, or eighty acres as heretofore.

In case of a party desiring to avail himself thereof, you will require him to file the usual homestead application for the tract desired, if legally liable to entry, to make affidavit according to the form hereto annexed, instead of the usual homestead affidavit, and on doing so allow him to make payment of the $10 fee stipulated in the act of 20th May, 1862, and the usual commissions on the price of the land at $2.50 per acre, the entry to be regularly numbered and reported to this office in your monthly homestead returns.

Regarding settlement and cultivation, the requirements of the law in this class of entries are the same as in other homestead entries.

Very respectfully your obedient servant,

JOSEPH S. WILSON,
Commissioner, Register, and Receiver.

———

AFFIDAVIT.

LAND OFFICE, AT ——

——, of ——, having filed my application No. ——, for an entry under the provisions of the act of Congress, approved May 20, 1862, and desiring to avail myself of the 25th section of the act of July 15, 1870, in regard to land held at the double minimum price of $2.50 per acre, do solemnly swear that I am the identical ——, who was a —— in the company* commanded by Captain ——, in the —— regiment of ——, commanded by ——, in the war of 1861 ; that I continued in actual service for ninety days, and have remained loyal to the Government; that said application, No. ——, is made for my exclusive benefit, and for the purpose of actual settlement and cultivation, and not directly or indirectly for the use or benefit of any other person or persons, and that I have not heretofore had the benefit of the Homestead law.

——— ———,

Sworn to and subscribed this —— day of ——, before

——— ———,

Register or Receiver of Land Office.

Approved :

[Signed]   J. D. COX, Secretary.

Department of the Interior, Aug. 8, 1870.

* Where the party was a regimental or staff officer, or was in a different branch of the service, the affidavit must be varied in form according to the facts of the case. 9

THE NEW NATURALIZATION LAW.

AN ACT TO AMEND THE NATURALIZATION LAWS AND TO PUNISH CRIMES
AGAINST THE SAME, AND FOR OTHER PURPOSES.

*Be it enacted by the Senate and House of Representatives of the United
States of America in Congress assembled,* That in all cases where any oath,
affirmation, or affidavit shall be made or taken under or by virtue of any
act or law relating to the naturalization of aliens, or in any proceedings
under such acts or laws, if any person or persons taking or making
such oath, affirmation, or affidavit, shall knowingly swear or affirm falsely, the same shall be deemed and taken to be perjury, and the person or
persons guilty thereof shall upon conviction thereof be sentenced to imprisonment for a term not exceeding five years and not less than one
year, and to a fine not exceeding one thousand dollars.

SEC. 2.—*And be it further enacted,* That if any person applying to
be admitted a citizen, or appearing as a witness for any such person, shall
knowingly personate any other person than himself, or falsely appear in
the name of a deceased person, or in an assumed or fictitious name, or if
any person shall falsely make, forge, or counterfeit any oath, affirmation,
notice, affidavit, certificate, order, record, signature, or other instrument,
paper, or proceeding required or authorized by any law or act relating to
or providing for the naturalization of aliens ; or shall utter, sell, dispose
of, or use as true or genuine, or for any unlawful purpose, any false,
forged, ante-dated, or counterfeit oath, affirmation, notice, certificate, order,
record, signature, instrument, paper, or proceeding as aforesaid ; or sell
or dispose of to any person other than the person for whom it was origin-
ally issued, any certificate of citizenship, or certificate showing any person to be admitted a citizen ; or if any person shall in any manner use
for the purpose of registering as a voter, or as evidence of a right to vote,
or otherwise, unlawfully, any order, certificate of citizenship, or certificate,
judgment, or exemplification, showing such person to be admitted to be a
citizen, whether heretofore or hereafter issued or made, knowing that
such order or certificate, judgment or exemplification has been unlawfully issued or made ; or if any person shall unlawfully use, or
attempt to use, any such order or certificate, issued to or in the
name of any other person, or in a fictitious name, or the name of
a deceased person ; or use, or attempt to use, or aid, or assist, or
participate in the use of any certificate of citizenship, knowing the same
to be forged, or counterfeit, or ante-dated, or knowing the same to have

been procured by fraud, or otherwise unlawfully obtained; or if any person, without any lawful excuse, shall knowingly have or be possessed of any false, forged, ante-dated, or counterfeit certificate of citizenship, purporting to have been issued under the provisions of any law of the United States relating to naturalization, knowing such certificate to be false, forged, ante-dated, or counterfeit, with intent unlawfully to use the same; or if any person shall obtain, accept, or receive any certificate of citizenship known to such person to have been procured by fraud, or by the use of any false name, or by means of any false statement made with intent to procure, or to aid in procuring, the issue of such certificate, or known to such person to be fraudulently altered or ante-dated; or if any person who has been or may be admitted to be a citizen shall, on oath or affirmation, or by affidavit, knowingly deny that he has been so admitted, with intent to evade or avoid any duty or liability imposed or required by law, every person so offending shall be deemed and adjudged guilty of felony, and, on conviction thereof, shall be sentenced to be imprisoned and kept at hard labor for a period not less than one year nor more than five years, or be fined in a sum not less than three hundred dollars nor more than one thousand dollars, or both such punishments may be imposed, in the discretion of the court. And every person who shall knowingly and intentionally aid or abet any person in the commission of any such felony, or attempt to do any act hereby made felony, or counsel, advise, or procure, or attempt to procure the commission thereof, shall be liable to indictment and punishment in the same manner and to the same extent as the principal party guilty of such felony, and such person may be tried and convicted thereof without the previous conviction of such principal.

SEC. 3.—*And be it further enacted,* That any person who shall knowingly use any certificate of naturalization heretofore granted by any court, or which shall hereafter be granted, which has been, or shall be, procured through fraud or by false evidence, or has been or shall be issued by the clerk, or any other officer of the court without any appearance and hearing of the applicant in court and without lawful authority; and any person who shall falsely represent himself to be a citizen of the United States, without having been duly admitted to citizenship, for any fraudulent purpose whatever, shall be deemed guilty of a misdemeanor, and upon conviction thereof in due course of law, shall be sentenced to pay a fine of not exceeding one thousand dollars, or be imprisoned not exceeding two years, either or both, in the discretion of the court taking cognizance of the same.

SEC. 4.—*And be it further enacted,* That the provisions of this act shall apply to all proceedings had or taken, or attempted to be had or taken, before any court in which any proceeding for naturalization shall be commenced, had, or taken, or attempted to be commenced; and the courts of the United States shall have jurisdiction of all offenses under the provisions of this act, in or before whatsoever court or tribunal the same shall have been committed.

SEC. 5.—*And be it further enacted,* That in any city having upward of twenty thousand inhabitants, it shall be the duty of the judge of the circuit court of the United States for the circuit wherein said city shall be, upon the application of two citizens, to appoint in writing for each election district or voting precinct in said city, and to change or renew said appointment as occasion may require, from time to time, two citizens resident of the district or precinct, one from each political party, who, when so designated, shall be, and are hereby, authorized to attend at all times and places fixed for the registration of voters, who, being registered, would be entitled to vote for representative in Congress, and at all times and places for holding elections of representatives in Congress, and for counting the votes cast at said elections, and to challenge any name proposed to be registered, and any vote offered, and to be present and witness throughout the counting of all votes, and to remain where the ballot boxes are kept at all times after the polls are open until the votes are finally counted; and said persons or either of them shall have the right to affix their signature or his signature to said register for purposes of identification, and to attach thereto, or to the certificate of the number of votes cast, any statement touching the truth or fairness thereof which they or he may ask to attach ; and any one who shall prevent any person so designated from doing any of the acts authorized as aforesaid, or who shall hinder or molest any such person in doing any of the said acts, or shall aid or abet in preventing, hindering or molesting any such person in respect of any such acts, shall be guilty of a misdemeanor, and on conviction shall be punished by imprisonment not less than one year.

SEC. 6.—*And be it further enacted,* That in any city having upward of twenty thousand inhabitants, it shall be lawful for the marshal of the United States for the district wherein said city shall be, to appoint as many special deputies as may be necessary to preserve order at any election at which representatives in Congress are to be chosen; and said deputies are hereby authorized to preserve order at such elections, and to arrest for any offence or breach of the peace committed in their view.

SEC. 7.—*And be it further enacted,* That the naturalization laws are hereby extended to aliens of African nativity and to persons of African descent.

Approved, July 14, 1870.

THE PATENT OFFICE.

THE following statistics show the growth of the patent system for thirty years in the United States. The statistics for 1869 are the latest yet issued from the office.

Years.	Applications.	Patents issued.	Receipts.	Expenditures.
1840	765	228	$38,056.51	$39,020.67
1845	1,246	502	51,076.14	39,395.65
1850	2,193	995	86,927.05	80,100.95
1855	4,435	2,024	216,459.35	179,540.33
1860	7,653	4,819	256,352.59	252,890.20
1865	10,664	6,616	348,791.84	274,199.23
1869	19,271	13,936	693,145.31	486,430.74

THE TOBACCO CROP.

COMPARATIVE ESTIMATES OF THE GROWTH WITHIN THE UNITED STATES.

LEAF.

		1868	1869	1870
Virginia	Hhds.	47,000	38,000	50,000
Maryland	"	30,000	25,000	30,000
Ohio	"	16,000	15,000	18,000
Kentucky	"	90,000	70,000	90,000
Other Western	"	30,000	30,000	40,000
Total	"	213,000	178,000	228,000

SEED-LEAF.

		1865	1866	1867	1868	1869	1870
Massachusetts and Conn.	Cases	25,000	30,000	16,000	30,000	34,000	32,000
New York	"	8,000	6,000	4,000	4,000	10,000	11,000
Pennsylvania	"	8,000	5,000	3,000	7,000	13,500	14,000
Ohio	"	12,000	20,000	10,000	13,500	13,500	15,000
Western	"	5,000	5,000	1,500	1,500	4,000	7,000
Total	"	58,000	66,000	34,500	56,000	75,000	79,000

FOREIGN GOVERNMENTS.

PRESENT RULERS, POPULATION, ETC.

ARGENTINE Republic. Capital, Buenos Ayres. President, Gen. Sarmiento; Vice-President, Don Alsina. Population, 1,800,000; square miles, 1.100,000.

Austro-Hungarian Empire. Capital, Vienna. Emperor of Austria and King of Hungary, Francis Joseph I. Minister of Foreign Affairs, Count Andrassy. Population, 35,950,000; square miles, 240,381.

Belgium. Capital, Brussels. King Leopold II. Minister of State, Baron d'Anethan. Population, 169,249; square miles, 2,357.

Bolivia, Republic of. Capital, Chuquisaca. President, M. Morales. Population, 1,987,352; square miles, 374,480.

Brazil, Empire of. Capital, Rio de Janeiro. Emperor, Pedro II. Minister of Foreign Affairs, Councilor Manoel Francisco Carreia. Population, 11,790,000; square miles, 3,231,047.

Borneo. Capital, Borneo. Sultan, Abdul Mumem. Rajah of Sarawak, Charles Brooke. Population, 25,000,000; square miles, 300,000.

British Empire. Capital, London. Queen, Victoria I. Prime Minister, W. E. Gladstone. Population, 245,539,733; area, 4,605,302 square miles.

Chili, Republic of. Capital, Santiago. President, Don Jose Joachim Joaquin Perez. Population, 2,081,945; square miles, 132,624.

China. Capital, Pekin. Emperor, Tung Chih. Envoys Extraordinary and Minister Plenipotentiary to the Treaty Powers, H. E. Chih Kang and H. E. Sun Chia Ku. Population, 460,000,000; square miles, 4,695,334.

Costa Rica. Capital, San José. Provisional President, General Guardia. Population, 150,000; square miles, 21,495.

Denmark. Capital, Copenhagen. King, Christian IX. Minister of Foreign Affairs, Baron Rosenorn Lehn. Population, 1,732,115; square miles, 14,616.

Ecuador, Republic of. Capital, Quito. President, Don Gabriel Garcia Moreno. Population, 1,110,000; square miles, 218,984.

Egypt. Capital, Cairo. Khedive, Ismail Pasha. Minister of Foreign Affairs, Nubar Pasha. Population, 5,800,000; sq. miles, 175,800.

Feejee Islands. King, Thako-mbau. Population about 200,000.

France. Capital, Paris. President, M. Louis Adolphe Thiers. Minister of Foreign Affairs, Compte de Rémusat. Population estimated at 36,500,000; area before the war, 405,488 square miles.

Colonies. The colonies and foreign possessions of France in Africa and Algeria are Senegal and its dependencies, the Islands of Bourbon (Réunion), and St. Marie in the Indian Ocean. Total possessions in Africa cover an area of 95,700 square miles, with a population of 473,500 souls. In America are the Islands of Martinique and Guadaloupe; French Guiana, Cayenne, etc ; with St. Pierre and Miquelon near Newfoundland; forming together an area of 80,000 square miles, with a population of 302,000. In Asia, the Indian settlements of Pondicherry, Mahé, etc., comprise altogether 10,800 square miles, with a population of 2,221,000. In the Pacific Ocean are two groups,—the Marquesas and Tahiti, and New Caledonia,—the whole forming an area of 9,560 sq. miles, with 84,000 inhabitants.

German Empire. Capital, Berlin. Emperor, William. Minister of Foreign Affairs and Chancellor of the North German Confederation, Otto, Prince Bismarck Schonhausen. Population of Prussia proper, 3,090,960; square miles, 1,179,004.

Anhalt, Duchy of. Duke, Leopold. Population, 197,041; square miles, 1,459.

Baden. Capital, Carlsruhe. Grand Duke, Frederick I. Minister of State, Rudolfson Freydorf. Population, 1,434,970; square miles, 5,912.

Bavaria. Capital, Munich. King, Louis II. Minister of State, Count von Hegnenberg Dux. Population, 4,824,421; square miles, 29,371.

Brunswick, Duchy of. Capital, Brunswick. Duke, William I. Population, 302,792 ; German square miles, 1,525.

Hesse-Darmstadt. Capital, Darmstadt. Grand Duke, Louis III. Minister of State, Baron de Lindelof. Population, 823,138; German square miles, 139,064.

Mecklenburg Schwerin. Capital, Schwerin. Grand Duke, Frederick Francis II. Minister of State, Le Comte H. F. C. de Bassewitz. Population, 560,618 ; square miles, 4,701.

Mecklenburg Strelitz. Capital, New Strelitz. Grand Duke, Frederick William I. Population, 98,770; square miles, 997.

Oldenburg, Grand Duchy of. Capital, Oldenburg. Grand Duke, Peter I. Population, 315,622; square miles, 2,417.

Saxony. Capital, Dresden. King, John I. Minister of Foreign Affairs, Baron Richard von Friesen. Population, 2,423,401 ; square miles, 5,705.

Saxe-Coburg and Gotha, Duchies of. Capital, Gotha. Duke, Ernest II. Population, 168,735; square miles, 790.

The Hanse Towns. The Hanse towns comprise the three republics of Hamburg, Bremen, and Lubec, and embrace an area of 482 square miles, and a population of 465,262.

Wurtemburg. Capital, Stuttgardt. King, Charles. Minister of Foreign Affairs, Baron de Varnbuler. Population, 1,778,396; square miles, 7,568.

Total population of German Empire, 50,767,142.

Greece. Capital, Athens. King, George I. Minister of Foreign Affairs, M. Zaimis, who is also Prime Minister. Population, 1,346,522; square miles, 19,353.

Guatemala, Republic of. Capital, Guatemala. President, Marshal de Comp. Vincento Cerna. Minister of Foreign Affairs, Senor Zavala. Population, 1,180,000; square miles, 44,788.

Hayti, Republic of. Capital, Port au Prince. President, General Nissage Saget. Minister for Foreign Affairs, T. Archim. Population, 572,000; square miles, 10,205.

Honduras, Republic of. Capital, Comayagua. President, Gen. José Maria Medina. Population, 500,000; square miles, 64,680.

Italy. Capital, Rome. King, Victor Emmanuel II. Minister of Foreign Affairs, Chev. Visconti Venosta. Population, 25,766,217; square miles, 148,389.

Japan. Capital, Miaco. Mikado. Population, 35,000,000; square miles, 149,399.

Liberia. Capital, Monrovia President, Edward James Roye. Secretary of State, John N. Lewis. Population, 20,000; square miles, 30,000.

Madagascar. Capital, Tananarivo. Queen, Ranavolo II. Population, 4,700,000; square miles, 240,000.

Mexico, Republic of. Capital, Mexico. President, Benito Juarez. Population, 8,137,853; square miles, 773,144.

Morocco. Principal capital, Fez. Sultan, Sidi Mohammed. Population, 8,000,000; square miles, 225,000.

Muscat. Capital, Muscat. Sovereign, Azan bin Ghes. Population, 60,000; square miles, 176,000.

Netherlands. Capital, Amsterdam. King, William III. Minister of Foreign Affairs, T. L. H. A. Baron Gericke van Herwijnen. Population, 24,053,481; square miles, 128,098.

New Grenada, Republic of. Capital, Bogota. President, General E. Salgar. Population, 3,000,000; square miles, 357,179.

Nicaragua, Republic of. Capital, Managua. President, Fernando Guzman. Minister of Foreign Affairs, T. Ayon. Population, 400,000; square miles, 58,169.

Orange River (Free State). Capital, Bloem Fontein. President, J. H. Brand. Population, 30,000; square miles, 2,260.

Paraguay, Republic of. Capital, Asuncion. President, M. Rivarola. Population, 1,400,000 ; square miles, 86,000.

Persia. Capital, Teheran. Sovereign, Shah Nasser-ed-Deen. Population, 5,000,000; square miles, 562,344.

Peru, Republic of. Capital, Lima. President, Col. José Balta. Foreign Minister, José J. Loaiza. Population, 3,374,000; square miles, 510,107.

Portugal. Capital, Lisbon. King, Dom Luis I. President of the Council, Fontes Pereira de Mello. Population, 3,987,867; square miles, 36,510 ; pop. including colonies, 8,232,541 ; square miles, 562,451.

Russia. Capital, St. Petersburg. Emperor, Alexander II. Minister of Foreign Affairs, Prince Alexander Gortchakoff. Population, 77,008,- 448; square miles, 7,862,568.

Sandwich Islands. Capital, Honolulu. King, Kamehameha. Minister of Foreign Affairs, Hon. C. C. Harris. Population, 62,000; square miles,6,500.

San Salvador, Republic of. Capital, San Salvador. President, Dr. Francis Duenas. Population, 750,000; square miles, 7,335.

Siam. Capital, Bangkok. First King, Chau Fa Chula Longkorn. Second King, Kromamum Bawarawichai Chau. Population, 6,300,000; square miles, 310,000.

Spain. Capital, Madrid. King, Amadeus. President of the Council and Minister of the Interior, Admiral Topete. Population, 16,641,984; population, including colonies, 21,286,675 ; square miles, 176,480; including colonies, 318,708.

Santo Domingo, Republic of. Capital, Santo Domingo. President, Gen. B. Baez. Minister of Foreign Affairs, H. M. Gautier. Population, 136,500 ; square miles, 17,826.

Sweden and Norway (Scandinavia). Capitals, Stockholm and Christiania. King, Charles XV. Minister of Foreign Affairs, Count B. Platen. Population, 5,865,053; square miles, 292,440.

Switzerland, Republic of. Capital, Berne. President of Federal Council, Dr. Emil Welti. Vice-President of Federal Council, Dr. Karl Schink. President of Federal Assembly, Andolf Brunner. Population, 2,510,494; square miles, 15,722.

Turkey. Capital, Constantinople. Sultan, Abdul Aziz. Minister of Foreign Affairs, Mahmud Pasha. Population, 40,000,000; square miles, 1,917,472. Wallachia, a province in the north-east of European Turkey, comprises an area of 25,000 square miles, and a population of 2,500,000. Moldavia, situated in the north-eastern extremity of European Turkey, comprises an area of 17,020 square miles, and a population of about 1,300,000.

United States of America. Capital, Washington. President, Ulysses S. Grant. Secretary of State, Hamilton Fish. Population, 38,555,- 983; square miles, 3,578,392. 10

Uruguay, Republic of. Capital, Monte Video. President, General Lorenzo Battle. Population, 400,000; square miles, 66,716.

Venezuela, Republic of. Capital, Caracas. President, General A. Guzman Blanco. Vice-President, General Ignacio Pulido. Population, 2,194,433; square miles, 368,235.

Zanzibar. Capital, ———. Sultan. Said Medjid. Population, 380,000; square miles, 1,450.   ⸱ .

DOMINION OF CANADA.⸴ CAPITAL, OTTAWA.

Population, 4,018,099.

Civil Establishment.—Governor General, Rt. Hon. Lord Dufferin; Governor's Secretary, Dennis Godley, Esq.; Military Secretary, Lieut. Col. C. J. M. McNeill, V.C.; Prov. A. D. C. Col. Irvine · A. D. C., Lt. Hon. W. A. W. Ponsonby.

Privy Council.—President of Council, Hon. C. Tupper, G.B.; Minister of Justice and Attorney General, Hon. Sir J. A. MacDonald, K.C.B., D. C. L. Premier; Minister of Militia, Hon. Sir G. E. Cartier; C B., Bt.; Minister of Customs, Hon. S. L. Tilley, C.B ; Minister of Finance, Hon. Sir Francis Hincks; Minister of Public Works, Hon. H. L. Langevin, C.B.; Minister of Inland Revenue, Hon. Alexander Morris ; Secretary of State for the Province, Hon. Joseph Howe ; Minister of Marine and Fisheries, Hon. Peter Mitchell ; Postmaster General, Hon. Alexander Campbell; Minister of Agriculture, Hon. Chris. Dunkin; Secretary of State of Canada, Superintendent-General of Indian Affairs, and Reg.-Gen., Hon. J. C. Aikins ; Receiver-General, Hon. Jean C. Chapais; Clerk of Privy Council, Wm. H. Lee; Lieutenant-General Commanding Forces in British North America, Lieut.-Gen. Sir Charles Hastings Doyle, K.C.M.G.; Military Secretary, Lieut. Col. Earle.

Ontario. Capital, Toronto. Population, 70,000. President of the Council, Blake ; Treasurer, McKenzie; Attorney General, Crooks; Minister of Public Works, McKellar ; Minister of Crown Lands, Scott; Provincial Secretary, Gow.

Quebec. Capital, Quebec. Population, 60,000. Lieut. Governor, Sir N. F. Belleau, Kt.; Premier, Hon. P. J. O. Chaveau; Treasurer, Hon. J. G. Robertson ; Attorney General, Hon. G. Ouimet ; Solicitor General, Hon. G. Irvine ; Commissioner of Crown Lands, J. O. Beaubien ; Commissioner of Agriculture, Hon. L. Archambault; Chief Justice Queens Bench, Hon. J. F. J. Duval ; Chief Justice Supreme Court, Hon. W. C. Meredith.

New Brunswick. Capital, Fredericton. Population of Province, 311,691. Lieut. Governor, Hon. L. Allen Wilmot, D.C.L. ; Private Secretary, Samuel Adams, Esq. ; Provincial Secretary, Hon. J. A. Beckwith; Chief Justice, Hon. William J. Ritchie ; Attorney General, Hon. George E. King.

Nova Scotia. Capital, Halifax. Population of Province, 388,000. Lt. Gov., Lieut. General Sir C. H. Doyle, K.C.M.G.; Private Secretary, Harry Moody, Esq.; Chief Justice, Sir Wm. Young; Judge in Equity, Hon. J. W. Johnston; Puisne Judges, Hons. E. M. Dodd, W. F. Desbarres, L. M. Wilkins, J. W. Ritchie, and Jonathan McCully; Attorney General, Hon. Martin J. Wilkins; Provincial Secretary, Hon. W. B. Vail.

DIFFERENCE OF TIME.

WHEN it is 12 o'clock at noon at New York City, it will be morning at all places west of New York, and afternoon at all places east, as in the annexed table.

WEST.

Place.	Morning. H. M. S.	Place	Morning. H. M. S.	Place.	Morning. H. M. S.
Acapulco, Mexico....	10 16 48	Little Rock, Ark....	10 47 16	Sacramento, Cal	8 56 44
Auburn, N. Y........	11 50 12	Louisville, Ky.......	10 14 4	St. Augustine, Fla...	11 29 44
Augusta, Ga.	11 28 24	Mexico, Mex........	10 19 44	St. Louis, Mo........	10 55 4
Baltimore, Md	11 49 38	Milledgeville, Ga....	11 22 45	St. Paul, Minn.......	10 43 45
Burlington, N. J....	11 56 34	Milwaukee, Wis....	11 4 16	San Antonio, Texas..	10 22 8
Buffalo, N. Y.......	11 40 24	Mobile, Ala.........	11 0 2	San Diego, Cal......	9 7 11
Charleston, S. C.....	11 36 22	Monterey, Mex......	10 14 22	San Francisco, Cal..	8 46 19
Chicago, Ill..........	11 6 2	Monterey, Cal	8 48 35	Santa Fe, N. Mex ..	9 51 59
Cincinnati, O........	11 18 16	Nashville, Tenn....	11 8 48	Santa Cruz, W.I....	8 48 4
Columbus, O	11 23 52	Natchez, Miss.......	10 50 26	Savannah, Ga........	11 31 32
Dayton, O...........	11 19 20	Newark, N. J.......	11 59 24	Scarboro Har., W. T.	8 37 36
Detroit, Mich........	11 23 54	Newbern, N. C.....	11 47 44	Springfield, Ill.......	10 57 52
Dover, Del...........	11 54 4	New Orleans, La....	10 56 4	Tallahassee, Fla.....	11 17 40
Ewing Harbor, O. T.	8 38 9	Norfolk, Va	11 50 49	Tampico, Mex.......	10 24 37
Ft. Leavenworth, Kan	10 37 8	Pensacola, Fla.......	11 8 0	Toronto, C. W.......	11 38 38
Galveston, Texas.....	10 36 58	Petersburg, Va......	11 46 44	Trenton, N. J.......	11 57 28
Geneva, N. Y........	11 48 44	Philadelphia, Pa....	11 55 25	Tuscaloosa, Ala......	11 5 16
Harrisburg, Pa.......	11 47 53	Pittsburgh, Pa.......	11 35 56	Utica, N. Y.........	11 55 12
Honolulu, S. I	6 24 8	Point Hudson, W. T.	7 45 6	Vera Cruz, Mex.....	10 31 30
Huntsville, Ala.......	11 8 16	Princeton, N.J......	11 57 26	Vincennes, Ind.......	11 6 24
Indianapolis, Ind....	11 11 44	Racine, Wis	11 5 23	Washington, D. C...	11 47 53
Jackson, Miss........	10 55 32	Raleigh, N.C.......	11 40 52	Wheeling, W. Va....	11 33 16
Jefferson, Mo	10 47 32	Richmond, Va.......	11 46 15	Wilmington, N. C...	11 43 24
Key West, Fla.......	11 28 54	Rochester, N. Y	11 44 40	Wilmington, Del....	11 54 12
Knoxville, Tenn......	11 20 28	Sacketts Harbor, N.Y	11 52 16	Yorktown, Va.......	11 49 48

EAST.

Place.	Afternoon. H. M. S.	Place.	Afternoon. H. M. S.	Place.	Afternoon. H. M. S.
Albany, N. Y........	0 1 6	Halifax, N. S	0 41 38	Paris, France........	5 5 26
Augusta, Me........	0 16 44	Hamburg, Ger.......	5 35 58	Portland, Me........	0 15 10
Bangor, Me.........	0 26 56	Hartford, Conn......	0 5 21	Providence, R. I.....	0 10 25
Berlin, Prus........	5 49 39	London, Eng........	4 55 41	Quebec, Canada....	0 11 0
Boston, Mass	0 11 50	Lowell, Mass........	0 10 48	Rome, Italy	5 45 59
Constantinople, Tur.	6 52 0	Middletown, Conn...	0 5 28	St. Petersburg, Rus..	6 57 18
Dublin, Ireland......	4 30 42	Montreal, L. C......	0 1 44	Stockholm, Sweden..	6 8 18
Edinburgh, Scotland.	4 43 21	New Haven, Conn...	0 4 23	Vienna, Austria.....	6 1 37
Fredericton, N. B...	0 29 4				

THE CITIES OF THE WORLD.

THE following table gives the population of the leading cities of the world, according to the most recent statistics.

Name.	Population.	Name.	Population.
London	3,214,000	Liverpool	520,000
Yeddo	2,900,000	Moscow	420,000
Paris	1,950,000	Brooklyn	396,300
Pekin	1,700,000	Glasgow	401,000
Constantinople	1,350,000	Madrid	390,000
New York	944,710	Dublin	362,000
Berlin	804,000	Manchester	350,000
St. Petersburg	667,000	Lisbon	340,000
Philadelphia	674,022	St. Louis	312,963
Vienna	640,000	Chicago	298,983
Naples	600,000	Baltimore	267,354

THE INDIVIDUAL STATES OF THE UNION.

HISTORICAL AND STATISTICAL TABLE OF THE UNITED STATES OF NORTH AMERICA.

[*Note.*—The whole area of the United States, including water surface of lakes and rivers, is nearly equal to four million square miles, embracing the Russian purchase.]

The thirteen original States.	When first settled.	Area in square miles.	* Population, 1870
New Hampshire	1623	9,280	318,300
Massachusetts	1620	7,800	1,457,351
Rhode Island	1636	1,306	217,353
Connecticut	1633	4,750	537,454
New York	1613	47,000	4,382,759
New Jersey	1624	8,320	906,096
Pennsylvania	1681	46,000	3,521,791
Delaware	1627	2,120	125,015
Maryland	1634	11,124	780,894
Virginia—East and West	1607	61,352	1,667,177
North Carolina	1650	50,704	*1,071,361
South Carolina	1670	34,000	705,606
Georgia	1733	58,000	1,184,109

* The total population of the United States in 1860 was, in round numbers, 31,500,000. In 1865 it is estimated that the population was 35,500,000, including the inhabitants of the Territories, estimated at 360,000 persons on January 1, 1865. The Census of 1870 made the whole number about 39,000,000; at the end of the present century it will be, probably, 103,000,000.

THE INDIVIDUAL STATES OF THE UNION—continued.

States admitted	When settled.	Act organizing Territory.	United States statutes vol.	pp.	Act admitting State.	United States statutes vol.	page.	Area in square miles.	Population, 1870.
Kentucky......	1774	....	...	....	Feb. 4, 1791	1	189	37,680	1,323,264
Vermont........	1724	....	...	....	Feb. 18, 1791	1	191	a 10,212	330,585
Tennessee......	1756	....	...	....	June 1, 1796	1	491	45,600	1,258,326
Ohio	1788	Ordin'e of 1787	...	....	April 30, 1802	2	173	39,964	2,675,468
Louisiana......	1699	March 3, 1805	2	331	April 8, 1812	2	701	a 41,346	734,420
Indiana........	1730	May 7, 1800	2	58	Dec. 11, 1816	3	399	33,809	1,668,169
Mississippi	1540	April 7, 1798	1	549	Dec. 10, 1817	3	472	47,156	842,056
Illinois........	1683	Feb'ry 3, 1809	2	514	Dec. 3, 1818	3	536	a 55,410	2,567,036
Alabama.......	1713	March 3, 1817.	3	371	Dec. 14, 1819	3	608	50,722	996,175
Maine	1623	....	...	....	March 3, 1820	3	544	a 35,000	630,423
Missouri	1763	June 4, 1812	2	743	March 2, 1821	3	645	65,350	1,725,658
Arkansas......	1685	March 2, 1819	3	493	June 15, 1836	5	50	52,198	486,103
Michigan	1670	Jan'ry 11, 1805	2	309	Jan. 26, 1837	5	144	a 56,451	1,184,653
Florida	1565	March 30, 1822	3	654	March 3, 1845	5	742	59,268	189,953
Iowa...........	1778	June 12, 1838	5	235	March 3, 1845	5	742	55,045	1,181,309
Texas..........	1694	....	...	....	Dec. 29, 1845	9	108	274,356	795,590
Wisconsin	1669	April 20, 1836	5	10	March 3, 1847	9	178	53,924	1,055,501
California......	1769	....	...	....	Sept. 9, 1850	9	452	a188,981	556,208
Minnesota...,..	1654	March 3, 1849	9	403	Feb. 26, 1857	11	166	83,531	424,543
Oregon	1792	August 14, 1848	9	323	Feb. 14, 1859	11	383	95,274	90,878
Kansas	1849	May 30, 1854	10	277	Jan. 29, 1861	12	126	81,318	379,497
West Virginia..	1607	....	...	....	Dec. 31, 1862	12	633	23,000	447,943
e Nevada......	1848	March 2, 1861	12	209	Mar. 21, 1864	13	30	b 112,090	44,686
f Colorado.....	....	Feb'ry 28, 1861	12	172	....	..	..	a104,500	39,681
g Nebraska....	1852	May 30, 1854	10	277	March 1, 1867	13	47	75,995	116,888

Territories.	When settled.	Act organizing Territory.	United States statutes vol.	page	Area in square miles.	Population 1870.
Wyoming...................	1866	July 25, 1868......	15	178	97,883	9,118
New Mexico...............	1570	Sept. 9, 1850......	9	446	121,201	92,604
Utah.....................	1847	Sept. 9, 1850......	9	453	c 84,746	70,000
Washington...............	1840	March 2, 1853......	10	172	69,994	23,925
Dakota...................	1850	March 2, 1861......	12	239	j 150,932	14,181
Arizona	1600	Feb. 24, 1863......	12	664	d 113,916	9,658
Idaho....................	1862	March 3, 1863......	12	808	k 86,294	14,882
Montana..................	1862	May 26, 1864......	13	85	143,776	20,594
Indian	1832	....	..	...	68,991	......
h District of Columbia	1771 {	July 16, 1790...... March 3, 1791......	1 1	130 } 214 }	10 miles sq.	131,706
i North-western America, purchased by treaty of May 28, 1867	1799	July 27, 1868......	15	240	577,390	67,000

NOTES TO THE FOREGOING TABLE.

a. The areas of those States marked *a* are derived from geographical authorities, the public surveys not having been completely extended over them.

b. The present area of Nevada is 112,000 square miles, enlarged by adding one degree of longitude lying between the 37th and 42d degrees of north latitude, which was detached from the west part of Utah, and also north-western part of Arizona Territory, per act of Congress, approved May 5, 1866 (U. S. Laws, 1865 and 1866, p. 43), and assented to by the Legislature of the State of Nevada, January 18, 1867.

c. The present area of Utah is 84,476 square miles, reduced from the former area of 88,056 square miles by incorporating one degree of longitude on the east side, between the 41st and 42d degrees of north latitude, with the Territory of Wyoming, per act of Congress, approved July 25, 1868.

d. The present area of Arizona is 113,916 square miles, reduced from the former area of 126,141 square miles, by an act of Congress, approved May 5, 1866, detaching from the northwestern part of Arizona a tract of land equal to 12,225 square miles, and adding it to the State of Nevada. (U. S. Laws 1865 and 1866, p. 43.)

e. Nevada.—Enabling act approved March 24, 1864. (Statutes, vol. 13, p. 30.) Duly admitted into the Union. President's proclamation No. 22, dated October 31, 1864. (Statutes, vol. 13, p. 749.)

f. Colorado.—Enabling act approved March 21, 1863. (Statutes, vol. 13, p. 32.) Not yet admitted.

g. Nebraska.—Enabling act approved April 19, 1864. (Statutes, vol. 13, p. 47.) Duly admitted into the Union. See President's proclamation No. 9, dated March 1, 1867. (U. S. Laws 1866 and 1867, p. 4.)

h. That portion of the District of Columbia south of the Potomac River was retroceded to Virginia, July 9, 1846. (Statutes, vol. 9, p. 35.)

i. Boundaries.—Commencing at 54° 40' north latitude, ascending Portland Channel to the mountains, following their summits to 141° west longitude; thence north on this line to the Arctic Ocean, forming the eastern boundary. Starting from the Arctic Ocean west, the line descends Behring Straits, between the two islands of Krusenstern and Romanzoff, to the parallel of 65° 30', and proceeds due north without limitation into the same Arctic Ocean. Beginning again at the same initial point, on the parallel of 65° 30', thence, in a course southwest, through Behring Strait, between the Island of St. Lawrence and Cape Choukotski, to the 172° west longitude, and thence southwesterly, through Behring Sea, between the islands of Alton and Copper, to the meridian of 193° west longitude, leaving the prolonged group of the Aleutian Islands in the possessions now transferred to the United States, and making the western boundary of our country the dividing line between Asia and America.

j. The present area of Dakota is 150,932 square miles, reduced from the former area of 240,597 square miles, by incorporating seven degrees of longitude of the western part, between the 41st and 45th degrees of north latitude, with the Territory of Wyoming, per act of Congress, approved July 25, 1868.

k. The present area of Idaho is 86,294 square miles, reduced from the former area of 90,932 square miles by incorporating one degree of longitude on the east side, between the 42d and 44th degrees of north latitude with the Territory of Wyoming, per act of Congress, approved July 25, 1868.

THE STATES OF THE UNION.

STATES. (37.)	AREA. Square Miles.	POPULATION						Elect. Vot.	STATE GOVERNMENTS IN 1872.					
		White Populat'n 1860.	Col'd Popul'n 1860.	Total Popula'n 1860.	Total Populat'n 1870.	Incr. fr 1860 to 1870.	Incr. Per Cent.		CAPITALS.	GOVERNORS.	Term Expires.	Salary.	Legislature meets.	State Elections.
Alabama	50,722	526,271	437,770	964,201	1,002,000	37,199	3.92	8	Montgomery	Robt. B. Lindsay	Nov. 1872	$4,000	3 M. Nov.	Tu. a 1 M. Nov.
Arkansas	52,198	324,143	111,259	435,450	477,174	37,724	8.66	5	Little Rock	O. A. Hadley, Act	Jan. 1873	5,000	1 M. Jan.	1 Monday Nov.
California	188,981	358,110	4,086	379,994	549,608	169,814	44.69	6	Sacramento	Newton Booth	Dec. 1875	7,000	1 M. Dec.	1 Tuesd. Sept.
Connecticut	4,750	451,504	8,627	460,147	537,417	77,270	16.79	6	Hartf'd & N.H.	Marshall Jewell	May 1873	1,100	1 W. May.	1 Mond. April
Delaware	2,120	90,589	21,627	112,216	125,015	12,799	11.41	3	Dover	James Ponder	Jan. 1875	1,333	1 Tu. Jan.	1 Tuesd. April
Florida	59,268	77,747	62,677	140,424	189,995	49,571	35.30	3	Tallahassee	Harrison Reed	Jan. 1873	3,500	T.a 1 M.Jan	Tu a 1 M.Jan
Georgia	58,000	591,550	465,698	1,057,286	1,174,872	117,550	11.12	9	Atlanta	Jas. Milton Smith	Jan. 1872	4,000	2 W. Jan.	Tu a 1 M Nov.
Illinois	55,410	1,704,291	7,628	1,711,951	2,589,410	817,459	47.75	16	Springfield	John M. Palmer	Jan. 1873	1,500	1 W. Jan.	Tu a 1 M Nov.
Indiana	33,809	1,338,710	11,428	1,350,428	1,655,073	303,247	22.60	13	Indianapolis	Conrad Baker	Jan. 1873	3,000	1 W. Jan.	2 Tuesday Oct.
Iowa	55,045	673,779	1,069	674,913	1,181,359	506,446	75.04	8	Des Moines	C. C. Carpenter	Jan. 1874	3,000	2 Th. Jan.	2 Tuesday Oct.
Kansas	81,318	106,390	627	107,206	379,497	272,291	253.99	3	Topeka	James M. Harvey	Jan. 1873	2,000	2 Th. Jan.	Tu a 1 M Nov.
Kentucky	37,680	919,484	236,167	1,155,684	1,320,407	164,723	14.99	11	Frankfort	P. H. Leslie	Sept. 1875	5,000	1 M. Dec.	1 Monday Aug.
Louisiana	41,346	357,456	350,373	708,002	734,420	26,418	3.73	7	New Orleans	H. C. Warmoth	Jan. 1873	8,000	1 M. Jan.	1 Monday Nov.
Maine	35,000	626,947	1,327	628,279	628,719	440	.07	7	Augusta	Sidney Perham	Jan. 1873	2,500	1 W. Jan.	2 Monday Sept.
Maryland	11,124	515,918	171,131	687,049	790,095	103,046	15.00	7	Annapolis	Wm. P. White	Jan. 1876	3,600	1 W. Jan.	Tu a 1 M Nov.
Massachusetts	7,800	1,221,432	9,602	1,231,066	1,457,351	226,295	18.34	12	Boston	Wm. B. Washburn	Jan. 1873	5,000	1 W. Jan.	Tu a 1 M Nov.
Michigan	56,451	736,144	6,799	749,113	1,184,653	435,540	58.14	8	Lansing	Henry P. Baldwin	Jan. 1873	1,000	1 W. Jan.	Tu a 1 M Nov.
Minnesota	83,531	160,395	259	172,023	424,543	252,520	146.79	4	St. Paul	Horace Austin	Jan. 1874	3,000	T a 1 M Jan	Tu a 1 M Nov.
Mississippi	47,156	353,899	437,404	791,305	842,056	50,751	6.41	8	Jackson	R. C. Powers, Act	Jan. 1874	...	T a 1 M Jan	Tu a 1 M Nov.
Missouri	65,350	1,063,489	118,503	1,182,012	1,691,693	509,681	43.01	11	Jefferson City	B. Gratz Brown	Jan. 1873	2,500	L a 1 M De	Tu a 1 M Nov.
Nebraska	75,995	28,696	82	28,841	116,498	116,498	405.28	3	Lincoln	W. H. James, Act	Jan. 1873	1,000	T a 1 M Ja	Tu a 1 M Nov.
Nevada	81,539	6,810	45	6,857	42,456	42,456	319.16	3	Carson City	L. R. Bradley	Jan. 1873	6,000	1 M. Jan.	2 Tuesday Oct.
New Hampshire	9,280	325,579	494	326,073	317,710	8,633	12.56	5	Concord	Ezekiel Straw	June 1873	1,000	1 M. June	2 Tues. March
New Jersey	8,320	646,699	25,336	672,035	903,014	231,009	34.37	7	Trenton	Joel Parker	Jan. 1873	3,000	2 Tu. Jan.	Tu a 1 M Nov.
New York	47,000	3,831,590	49,005	3,880,735	4,370,046	850,111	12.63	33	Albany	John T. Hoffman	Jan. 1873	4,000	1 Tu. Jan.	Tu a 1 M Nov.
North Carolina	50,704	629,942	361,522	992,622	1,016,954	24,332	2.45	9	Raleigh	T.R.Caldwell, Act	Jan. 1873	5,000	1 Th. Nov.	1 Thurs. Aug.
Ohio	39,964	2,302,606	36,673	2,339,511	2,662,302	312,791	13.33	21	Columbus	Edward F. Noyes	Jan. 1874	4,000	1 M. Jan.	2 Tuesday Oct.
Oregon	95,274	52,160	128	52,465	90,923	38,413	73.64	3	Salem	L. F. Grover	Sept. 1874	1,500	2 M. Sept.	1 Monday June
Pennsylvania	46,000	2,849,259	56,949	2,906,115	3,511,543	605,328	20.83	26	Harrisburg	John W. Geary	Jan. 1873	5,000	1 Tu. Jan.	2 Tues. Oct.
Rhode Island	1,306	170,649	3,952	174,620	217,356	42,750	24.46	4	Newp't & Provid.	Seth Padelford	May 1873	1,000	May & Jan.	1 Wed. April
South Carolina	34,000	291,300	412,320	703,708	705,749	2,081	...	6	Columbia	Robert K. Scott	Jan. 1873	3,500	3 W. Oct.	1 Monday Nov.
Tennessee	45,600	826,722	283,019	1,109,801	1,225,937	116,136	10.46	10	Nashville	John C. Brown	Oct. 1873	4,000	1 M. Oct.	1 Monday Nov.
Texas	274,356	420,891	182,921	604,215	800,000	195,785	32.40	6	Austin	Edmund J. Davis	Jan. 1874	3,000	...	1 Tuesd. Sept.
Vermont	10,212	314,369	709	315,098	330,552	15,484	4.91	5	Montpelier	John W. Stewart	Oct. 1872	1,000	2 Th. Oct.	Tu a 1 M Nov.
Virginia	38,352	1,047,299	548,907	1,596,318	1,211,442	34,413	3.52	11	Richmond	Gilb't C. Walker	Jan. 1874	1,000	1 M. Dec.	Tu a 1 M Nov.
West Virginia	23,000			441,094	56,218	56,218	36.40	5	Charleston	John J. Jacob	Mar. 1873	2,000	1 Tu. Jan.	4 Thursd. Oct.
Wisconsin	53,924	773,693	1,171	775,881	1,055,501	279,021	36.40	8	Madison	C. C. Washburn	Jan. 1874	1,250	1 W. Jan.	Tu a 1 M Nov.

Total area (inclusive of Territories) 3,400,000 square miles. Population in 1850, 23,191,876; in 1860, 31,443,321; in 1870, 35,312,634. Whole number of Senators, 74; Congressmen, 244; total Electoral vote, 318. * Biennial Sessions and Elections. † Loss.

TERRITORIAL GOVERNMENTS.

Territories.	Capitals.	Governors.	Territories.	Capitals.	Governors.
Arizona....	Tucson....	A. P. K. Safford.	New Mexico.	Santa Fe ...	Marsh Giddings.
Colorado...	Denver....	Ed. M. McCook.	Utah	Salt Lake City.	George L. Woods.
Dakota	Yancton...	J. A. Burbank.	Washington.	Olympia.......	Edward S. Salomon
Idaho, ...	Boise	T. W. Bennett.	Wyoming .	Cheyenne	James A. Campbell
Indian	Tahlequah.	Cyrus Harris.	Dist.Colum'a	Washington...	Henry D. Cooke.
Montana...	Virg'a City	Benj. F. Potts.			

RAILROAD SYSTEM OF THE UNITED STATES.

The following tabulation shows the distribution of Mileage and cost of Railroads in the several States and Territories:

STATES AND TERRITORIES.	Length in Miles.		Cost of Road and Equipm.
	Total.	Open.	
Maine................................	972.01	810.31	$26,241,901
New Hampshire.......................	987.29	734.75	23,647,935
Vermont.............................	658.41	618.41	32,488,594
Massachusetts.......................	1,739.02	1,478.47	77,496,630
Rhode Island........................	135.80	135.80	4,805,996
Connecticut.........................	977.87	728.75	34,976,834
Total.......................	5,470.40	4,506.49	$199,658,090
New York............................	5,453.74	3,892.38	$234,049,545
New Jersey..........................	1,241.30	1,091.80	74,525,196
Pennsylvania........................	6,312.96	5,056.06	296,739,037
Delaware and East Maryland..........	588.64	390.14	10,059,092
Maryland (West).....................	840.34	495.49	34,721,367
West Virginia.......................	711.75	374.75	30,493,739
Total.......................	15,078.73	11,300.62	$680,589,976
Virginia............................	2,253.31	1,465.96	$53,386,858
North Carolina......................	1,574.17	1,178.17	32,164,298
South Carolina......................	1,438.17	1,138.67	32,813,588
Georgia.............................	2,313.70	1,932.70	44,322,919
Florida.............................	607.20	440.20	11,781,919
Total.......................	8,186.55	6,155.70	$174,519,582
Alabama.............................	2,120.00	1,396.00	$46,598,605
Mississippi.........................	1,117.80	977.80	33,208,839
Louisiana...........................	944.50	478.50	19,523,798
Texas...............................	4,071.50	665.50	22,050,000
Arkansas............................	1,054.00	286.00	8,798,000
Tennessee...........................	2,016.08	1,490.08	51,528,745
Kentucky............................	1,375.41	907.37	35,640,699
Total.......................	12,699.29	6,201.25	$217,348,686

RAILROAD SYSTEM OF THE UNITED STATES—continued.

STATES AND TERRITORIES.	Length in Miles.		Cost of Road and Equipm.
	Total.	Open.	
Ohio..	4,800.97	3,638.09	$192,538,214
Michigan.....................................	2,992.36	1,733.36	75,817,748
Indiana.......................................	4,865.20	3,277.60	135,957,186
Illinois.......................................	8,813.35	5,423.10	237,553,000
Wisconsin	3,142.20	1,475.20	59,833,881
Total.................................	24,614.08	15,547.35	$701,700,029
Missouri......................................	4,573.42	2,140.13	$106,663,464
Kansas..	3,698.00	1,501.00	56,723,700
Colorado......................................	1,268.00	368.00	17,400,000
Iowa..	4,472.25	2,550.25	111,978,000
Nebraska......................................	1,205.00	588.00	39,300,000
Wyoming Territory.............................	492.00	492.00	46,700,000
Minnesota.....................................	2,654.00	972.00	34,720,000
Dakota Territory..............................	700.00	....	300,000
Montana and Idaho Territory...................	600.00	....	....
Total.................................	19,662.67	8,611.38	$413,785,164
California....................................	3,293.60	996.60	$70,624,582
Nevada..	1,493.00	593.00	60,000,000
Utah Territory................................	404.00	364.00	49,000,000
Oregon	2,648.50	159.50	6,100,000
Washington Territory..........................	420.00	....	....
Total.................................	8,259.10	2,113.10	$185,724,582

RECAPITULATION.

STATES AND TERRITORIES.	Length in Miles.		Cost of Road and Equipm.
	Total.	Open.	
Northeastern States...........................	5,470.40	4,506.09	$199,658,090
Middle States.................................	15,078.73	11,300.62	680,589,976
Southeastern States...........................	8,186.55	6,155.70	174,519,582
Gulf and Southwestern States..................	12,699.29	6,201.25	217,348,686
Interior, east of Mississippi..................	24,614.08	15,547.35	701,700,029
" west " "	19,662.67	8,611.36	413,785,164
Pacific States................................	8,259.10	2,113.38	185,724,582
Total.................................	93,970.32	54,435.49	$2,573,526,109

In the following table is shown the increased Mileage and cost of Railroads in the several sections, during the year 1870:

	Miles of Road.		Cost of Road and Equipm.
	Projected.	Opened.	
Northeast.....................................	594.04	231.73	$ 9,853,292
Middle East...................................	531.54	509.53	21,971,451
Southeast.....................................	436.69	318.22	10,519,325
Gulf and Southwest............................	2,125.36	907.22	36,879,602
Interior, east of Mississippi..................	3,409.71	1,449.05	53,401,538
" west " "	6,421.10	1,731.05	66,416,600
Pacific	2,081.00	428.00	25,874,582
Total increase......................	15,606.44	5,574.80	$224,916,390

The average cost of Railroads in the United States, including the great overland lines which cost more than $100,000 per mile, or about 10 per cent. of the total cost of Railroads, is $47,277 per mile. But few of the great Eastern Trunk Roads have cost less than $80,000 to $100,000 per mile, while in the South the cost of Railroad building, notably in the Atlantic States, has not exceeded $20,000 to $25,000 per mile.

The progress of Railroad construction in the United States since 1827, in which year the Granite Railroad, at Quincy, Mass., was inaugurated, to the present time, is shown in the following table:

Year.	Miles Open.	Yearly Increase.	Year.	Miles Open.	Yearly Increase.
1827	3	...	1850	7,475	1,125
1828	3	...	1851	8,589	1,114
1829	28	25	1852	11,027	2,438
1830	41	13	1853	13,497	2,470
1831	54	13	1854	15,672	2,175
1832	131	77	1855	17,398	1,726
1833	576	445	1856	19,251	1,853
1834	762	186	1857	22,625	3,374
1835	918	156	1858	25,000	2,465
1836	1,102	184	1859	26,755	1,665
1837	1,431	329	1860	28,771	2,016
1838	1,843	412	1861	30,593	1,822
1839	2,220	477	1862	31,769	1,176
1840	2,797	577	1863	32,471	702
1841	3,319	522	1864	33,860	1,389
1842	3,877	558	1865	34,442	582
1843	4,174	297	1866	35,351	909
1844	4,311	137	1867	36,896	1,545
1845	4,522	211	1868	38,822	1,926
1846	4,870	348	1869	42,272	3,450
1847	5,336	466	1870	48,860	6,588
1848	5,682	346	1871	54,435	5,574
1849	6,350	668	1872		

EDUCATIONAL STATISTICS.

THE Public School statistics of the United States require a volume of themselves for their complete elucidation. We can only give aggregates of the most important items. ·

The number of children of school-age in 30 of the 37 States, in 1870, was 10,467,189. The number enrolled in 31 of the 37 States was 6,751,341. The average attendance in 24 out of 37 States, was 3,414,362. The number of schools in 29 States was 117,950. Nine States reported 320,000 children in private schools. In 30 States there were 181,574 teachers employed in the public schools; of these, 63,815 were male teachers, and 118,056 female teachers. Nevada paid the highest average salaries to both her male and ·female teachers, giving the former an average of $118.75 per month, and the latter $92.16, both in gold. North Carolina paid the smallest average to her male teachers—$20.50 per month—out of which they were required to pay $12, or thereabouts, for board. Maine paid the lowest wages to female teachers—$14 per month —though as this was in addition to the board, it was probably in reality higher than North Carolina or some of the other States.

In 25 States—all that reported—the average wages of male teachers were $51 per month, and of female teachers $33.12 per month.

The total annual income of the public schools in 31 States—embracing all except Georgia, Mississippi, Oregon, South Carolina, Texas, and Virginia, was nearly sixty-two millions of dollars. Of this immense sum, thirty-nine millions was raised in 24 States by taxation, nearly three millions was interest on permanent funds, and the remainder was derived from the sale of lands, rate-bills, and other sources.

The expenditures are divided into two classes, the one of current, the other of incidental expenditures. Under the first class come teachers' wages, fuel, &c. Under the second, the cost of sites, buildings, repairs, libraries, apparatus, and other objects. ·

The amount paid for teachers' wages in 22 States, in 1870, was $28,525,011.86. For fuel and insurance in 17 States, $4,567,307.97 was paid. In 25 States, $34,871,183.99 was paid for buildings, sites, and repairs. In 11 States, $424,000 was expended for libraries and apparatus.

The entire expenditure, reported from 30 States, is $58,018,371.48. Twenty-three States only report their school fund and its condition. The aggregate school funds of these States amount to $45,823,019,99. Several of the States not reporting have large funds, and it is probably within bounds to estimate the present value of the school funds of all the States as not less than $65,000,000.

The following table shows the number of colleges and collegiate institutions, instructors and students, in each State in the Union.

States.	No. of Coll'ges	No. of Instr's.	No. of Stud'ts.	States.	No. of Coll'ges	No. of Instr's.	No. of Stud'ts.
Alabama............	4	28	396	New Hampshire...	1	27	382
Arkansas..........	1	5	80	New Jersey........	6	75	934
California.........	13	125	1,891	New York	27	462	7,236
Connecticut.......	3	93	889	North Carolina....	15	67	1,449
Delaware	2	13	172	Ohio	35	292	5,780
Georgia...........	21	93	1,296	Oregon.......	4	16	526
Illinois......,.....	28	256	4,758	Pennsylvania	34	315	3,980
Indiana...........	19	176	3,905	Rhode Island......	1	14	217
Iowa..............	13	101	2,265	South Carolina....	7	50	461
Kansas...........	7	32	602	Tennessee..........	20	117	2,149
Kentucky.........	10	76	1,986	Texas.............	4	25	441
Louisiana.........	7	60	854	Vermont..........	4	38	379
Maine.............	4	44	473	Virginia...........	11	109	2,124
Maryland.........	10	128	1,121	West Virginia......	3	23	301
Massachusetts.....	6	140	1,350	Wisconsin.........	14	110	2,691
Michigan	7	81	1,470	Dist. of Columbia..	4	70	1,215
Minnesota........	2	14	342	Utah..............	1	...	296
Mississippi.......	5	24	572	Wash'n Territory..	1	3	80
Missouri..........	14	149	2,131				

Of scientific and professional schools in the United States, there are ninety-three *Theological Seminaries* having 384 instructors, and about 3,600 students; twenty-eight *Law Schools*, with 100 professors and about 1,800 students; fifty-nine *Regular Medical Schools*, with 440 or more professors, and about 7,000 students; five *Eclectic Medical Schools*, with about 35 professors and 325 students; one *Physio-Medical* or *Botanic School*, with 6 professors and 42 students; seven *Homœopathic*, with 65 professors and nearly 400 students; six *Dental Colleges*, with 39 professors and about 250 students; nineteen *Pharmaceutical Societies and Colleges*, with about 40 professors and perhaps 600 students. There are also eighty-two *Normal Schools* for the training of teachers, with about 230 teachers, and not far from 10,000 students; twenty-six *Agricultural and Scientific Schools*, and several others about to open, all largely endowed, and with about 200 professors and at least 2,000 students.

There are, moreover, 20 or more commercial or business colleges, giving a limited course of instruction generally only in topics relating to business. These have over 120 teachers and about 5,000 students.

There are 36 institutions for the instruction and training of deaf mutes, 22 for the blind, and 7 for the idiotic.

Of special schools and means of instruction, beside the Military Academy at West Point and the Naval Academy at Annapolis, there are very many. Most of our larger cities have one or more, many of them two or three Schools of Art, Academies of Design, and Schools of Instruction in Wood Engraving, Free Drawing, Water-color Painting, Architectural Drawing, and Sketching and Modeling from nature and life. Some of them, like the Cooper Union in New York, the Peabody Institute at Baltimore, and the Stevens Institute at Hoboken, are magnificent foundations, and furnish opportunity for the highest free education in art matters. There are also numerous schools of higher instruction in music, with eminent teachers and a large attendance.

Special schools for instruction in navigation, surveying, mining, metallurgy, chemistry, and civil engineering are also becoming numerous.

Most of the Mercantile Library Associations have classes for the instruction of their members in modern language, mechanics, higher mathematics, etc., and many of the Young Men's Christian Associations have also established such classes.

There are 308 of the Young Men's Christian Associations, with an aggregate of about 53,000 members, and more than three-fourths of them have libraries, some of them of considerable size.

Aside from these, and from the college libraries, there are 161 Public Libraries in the United States, containing from 1,200 to 190,000 volumes in each. The largest of these are the Library of Congress, 190,000 volumes; the Boston Public City Library, about 140,000; the Astor Library, in New York, of about the same size; the Boston Athenæum, over 100,000; the Mercantile Library, in New-York City, about 120,000; the Philadelphia Library Company, about 85,000; the New York State Library, at Albany, nearly 80,000.

EXPENSES PER HEAD OF THE STATES FOR SCHOOL PURPOSES.

The United States Commissioner gives some very interesting figures in regard to the annual expenditure in each State, for each child of school age. In the list Nevada stands first, California third, and Connecticut fourth. But in Nevada and California, a large proportion of the expense is caused by the erection of new school-houses, so that the table gives these States a better standing than they are entitled to. Excluding these two, and Massachusetts stands first and Connecticut second.

The following is the table showing the expenditure per head of the school population, excepting seven States.

Nevada	$19.17	Ohio	$6.48	Louisiana	$2.84
Massachusetts	16.45	Michigan	6.40	Delaware	2.70
California	11.44	New Jersey	6.38	Missouri	2.65
Connecticut	10.29	Rhode Island	6.20	Nebraska	2.65
Pennsylvania	7.86	Minnesota	5.71	Indiana	2.37
Illinois	7.83	Wisconsin	4.98	Alabama	1.49
Iowa	7.21	Maine	4.78	Tennessee	.91
New York	6.83	Maryland	4.50	Florida	.91
Vermont	6.47	New Hampshire	4.46	Kentucky	.73
Kansas	6.45	Arkansas	3.97	North Carolina	.48

REAL AND PERSONAL ESTATE VALUATION,

CAPITAL INVESTED IN MANUFACTURES, TRADE OR COMMERCE, AND RAILWAYS, IN 1870

THE following table shows the Real and Personal Estate Valuation, Capital invested in Trade or Commerce, also the cost of Railways, in the several States, in the year 1870.

M indicates the Capital invested in Manufactures; T that invested in Trade; C Commerce by land or sea.

States.	Valuation of Real Estate.	Valuation of Personal Est.	Capital invested in Manufactures, Trade or Commerce.		Miles of Railway.	Cost of Railways.
Maine...............	$217,331,891	$169,037,423	M.	$48,000,000	810.3	$26,241,901
New Hampshire....	160,315,6?0	128,711,143	"	55,500,000	734.8	23,647,935
Vermont............	13?,627,143	85,744,621	"	37,?23,000	618.4	32,488,594
Massachusetts......	1,03?,083,415	803,085,9?8	"	250,000,000	1,478.5	77,496,830
Rhode Island	293,758,000	55,483,713	"	45,000,000	135.8	4,805,996
Connecticut........	312,574,40?	135,380,750	"	166,800,000	728.8	34,976,834
New York..........	2,532,720,907	2,434,270,278	C. & M.	3,200,000,000	3,892.4	234,049,545
New Jersey.........	513,000,000	27?,000,000	M.	135,000,000	1,091.8	74,525,196
Pennsylvania.......	1,046,732,062	346,?91,498	C. & M.	1,320,?50,000	5,056.1	296,739,037
Delaware	47,385,614	20,185,693	M.	16,550,000	*390.1	10,059,092
Maryland..........	398,891,449	327,937,008	M. & C.	117,500,000	†495.5	34,723,367
Virginia...........	885,000,000	85,000,000	M. & T.	86,230,000	1,466.0	53,386,858
West Virginia......	98,780,000	41,000,000	C.	28,000,000	374.8	30,493,739
North Carolina.....	393,837,993	188,931,290	M.	15,000,000	1,178.2	32,164,298
South Carolina.....	358,785,191	219,081,837	M. & T.	35,500,000	1,138.7	32,813,582
Georgia	386,129,231	267,825,641	" "	51,325,000	1,932.7	44,322,919
Florida	16,329,106	15,447,680	M. & C.	13,000,000	440.2	11,781,919
Alabama...........	327,500,000	125,500,000	" "	45,000,000	1,396.0	46,598,605
Mississippi	167,000,000	49,380,000	M. & T.	21,300,000	977.8	33,208,839
Louisiana	317,612,5?3	294,861,247	C.	48,000,000	478.5	19,523,798
Texas..............	298,163,281	159,328,216	M. & T.	27,480,000	665.5	22,050,000
Arkansas..........	86,297,123	127,261,326	" "	13,287,000	286.0	8,798,000
Tennessee..........	276,163,137	168,237,191	" "	79,500,000	1,490.1	51,528,745
Kentucky..........	329,218,742	271,864,165	T.	256,000,000	907.4	35,640,699
Ohio	1,607,418,203	959,762,252	"	2,300,000,000	3,638.1	192,538,214
Indiana............	937,201,283	367,130,625	C.	1,400,000,000	3,277.6	135,957,186
Illinois............	1,346,587,734	342,407,041	"	2,000,000,000	5,423.0	237,553,000
Missouri	805,893,165	497,487,635	C. & M.	1,729,000,000	2,140.1	106,663,464
Kansas............	69,125,000	31,285,000	T.	114,000,000	1,501.0	56,723,700
Nebraska	14,160,000	30,895,796	M.	6,600,000	588.0	39,300,000
Iowa...............	322,561,061	171,971,191	M. & C.	325,000,000	2,550.3	111,978,000
Michigan	387,246,129	183,284,721	C. & M.	387,642,000	1,733.4	75,817,749
Wisconsin	360,000,000	138,000,000	M.	32,000,000	1,475.2	59,833,881
Minnesota	71,155,000	29,387,000	"	14,831,000	972.0	34,720,000
Nevada............	19,360,000	14,287,000	"	3,925,000	593.0	60,000,000
California..........	217,855,933	128,725,471	C. & M.	150,000,000	996.6	70,624,582
Oregon............	29,830,117	19,187,323	M.	11,350,000	159.5	6,100,000
Dist. of Columbia...	83,127,841	49,287,605	M. & T.	19,270,000	....	....
Territories.........	79,184,821	52,829,613	M.	21,362,000	1,224.0	113,400,000

*Delaware, and Eastern Shore, Maryland.

†Western Maryland.

RELIGIOUS STATISTICS OF THE UNITED STATES IN 1872.

Denominations and Sects.	Archbishops	Bishops, Superintendents, etc.	Clergymen	Dioceses, Conf'nc's, Synods, Classes, Associat'ns, Presbyteries, &c.	Churches, Congregations or Parishes	Church Edifices	Sittings	Members of Churches, Congregations or Parishes	Adherent Population	Value of Church Edifices	Contributions to Benevolent Objects and Church Purposes	Sunday Schools	Sunday School Scholars and Teachers	Additions to Membership during the Year	Academies and Seminaries of Denomination	Colleg's & Theol. Seminaries of Denomination	Newspap'rs and Periodicals of Denomination
Roman Catholics	7	60	3,907	60	4,781	4,176	1,990,514	3,758,000	4,000,000	60,965,566	8,796,000		300,000	195,000		57 } 62	99
Methodist Episcopal		13	21,234	72	13,373	11,769	3,576,180	1,307,134	5,700,000	52,614,501		16,912	1,410,906	116,934			28
" South		8	7,586	30	4,560	4,127	1,285,175	571,241	2,260,000	15,196,800	2,238,150	2,519	135,954	56,172	5	10	15
United Brethren in Christ		4	1,709	42	3,912	1,514	421,400	120,445	567,000	2,065,000	641,840			2,390			11
Other Methodists		21	10,986	155	7,129	4,628	1,473,000	773,125	3,140,000	6,187,650					13	55	4
Free Will Baptists			1,145		1,396	1,391	127,560	60,909	266,000	1,186,430				5,665	29	11	43
Regular Baptists			12,013	630	18,397	18,876	3,907,116	1,489,191	5,983,000	49,229,221	10,497,103	5,287	408,756	144,323	16		98
Disciples			1,797		2,476			467,223	1,672,000								6
Mennonites, Tunkers, Winebrenarians			950		990	760	131,250	88,000	275,000	605,285							
Seventh Day, Six Principle, Anti-Mission and other Baptists			700		860	430		70,000	200,000			601					3
Presb'n Ch. Unit'd Gen. Assemb.			4,795	192	4,616	4,430	1,798,900	455,374	2,510,000	38,167,250	9,097,706		470,817	49,948	23	45	26
Presbyterian Church South			1,096	66	1,518	1,989	387,000	87,529	425,000	9,785,340	1,034,390		50,355	8,475		3	2
Reformed Presbyterians, 3 sects			197	10	205	187	54,000	19,000	75,000	567,000					3		9
United Presbyterians			566	63	731	658	263,420	71,804	300,000	2,718,150	800,001		52,616	8,088	7	7	2
Cumberland Presbyterians			1,314	103	1,863	1,095	384,260	96,335	425,000	1,967,650			29,908	7,850	18	10	9
Reformed (German)			526	32	1,212	1,056	290,000	101,894	535,000	3,186,500	594,250	601	51,210	10,660	20	3	3
Reformed (Dutch)			560	34	470	448	228,300	42,483	342,000	3,976,500	1,227,657	518	51,169	6,046	16	24	12
Congregationalists			3,194	39	3,121	3,015	417,212	312,651	1,650,000	19,103,630	6,650,814	1,019	308,937	24,271	7	28	9
Protestant Episcopal		53	2,898	46	2,695	2,421	991,051	224,995	1,109,000	36,314,549	5,344,575		253,384	24,124	5	33	17
Lutherans		5	4,157	54	3,722	3,370	997,332	495,325	1,950,000	14,917,747	131,000			55,308	8	1	22
United Brethren (Moravians)			86	6	65	61	40,000	15,064	59,700	150,000	100,000		6,120		5	5	32
Unitarians			396	21	347	325	75,000	30,000	60,000	2,390,000	200,000			1,625	5	6	5
Christian Connection			3,000	40	5,000		131,600	300,000	600,000	3,975,000					8	3	13
Universalists			633	84	944	668	150,000	84,000	200,000	1,670,000			65,000	2,150	6	1	1
Friends (Orthodox)				10	540	512		57,405	225,000	500,000					3		2
Hicksite and Progressive Friends				8	74	88		40,000	120,000	470,000					1		
New Jerusalem Church, or Swedenborgians			63	9	210		10,000	5,000	25,000								9
Jews	3	241						50,000	80,000	3,950,000	63,000				17		7
Mormons								50,000	75,000						10		5
Spiritualists			150		165	88		100,000	500,000					2,150			10
Minor Sects not includ. elsewhere.								9,000	27,000	45,000							3
Deistical, Atheistical, Radical or Liberal Clubs.							10,000		250,000								5

CONSTITUTION OF THE UNITED STATES.

WE, the people of the United States, in order to form a more perfect Union, establish justice, insure domestic tranquility, provide for the common defense, promote the general welfare, and secure the blessings of liberty to ourselves and our posterity, do ordain and establish this Constitution of the United States of America:

ARTICLE I.—CONGRESS.

SECTION I.—*Legislative Powers.*

1. All legislative powers herein granted shall be vested in a Congress of the United States, which shall consist of a Senate and House of Representatives.

SECTION II.—*House of Representatives.*

1. The House of Representatives shall be composed of members chosen every second year by the people of the several States, and the electors in each State shall have the qualifications requisite for electors of the most numerous branch of the State Legislature.

Qualification of Members—Apportionment.

2. No person shall be a Representative who shall not have attained to the age of twenty-five years, and been seven years a citizen of the United States, and who shall not, when elected, be an inhabitant of that State in which he shall be chosen.

3. Representatives and direct taxes shall be apportioned among the several States which may be included within this Union, according to their respective numbers, which shall be determined by adding to the whole number of free persons, including those bound to service for a term of years, and excluding Indians not taxed, three fifths of all other persons. The actual enumeration shall be made within three years after the first meeting of the Congress of the United States, and within every subsequent term of ten years, in such manner as they shall by law direct. The number of Representatives shall not exceed one for every thirty thousand, but each State shall have at least one Representative; and until such enumeration shall be made, the State of *New Hampshire* shall be entitled to choose three, *Massachusetts* eight, *Rhode Island and Providence Plantations* one, *Connecticut* five, *New York* six, *New Jersey* four, *Pennsylvania*

eight, *Delaware* one, *Maryland* six, *Virginia* ten, *North Carolina* five, *South Carolina* five, and *Georgia* three.

4. When vacancies happen in the representation from any State, the Executive authority thereof shall issue writs of election to fill such vacancies.

5. The House of Representatives shall choose their Speaker and other officers, and shall have the sole power of impeachment.

SECTION III.—*Senate.*

1. The Senate of the United States shall be composed of two Senators from each State, chosen by the Legislature thereof for six years; and each Senator shall have one vote.

2. Immediately after they shall be assembled in consequence of the first election, they shall be divided as equally as may be into three classes. The seats of the Senators of the first class shall be vacated at the expiration of the second year, of the second class at the expiration of the fourth year, and of the third class at the expiration of the sixth year; so that one third may be chosen every second year; and if vacancies happen by resignation, or otherwise, during the recess of the Legislature of any State, the Executive thereof may make temporary appointments, until the next meeting of the Legislature, which shall then fill such vacancies.

3. No person shall be a Senator who shall not have attained to the age of thirty years, and been nine years a citizen of the United States, and who shall not, when elected, be an inhabitant of that State for which he shall be chosen.

4. The Vice-President of the United States shall be President of the Senate, but shall have no vote unless they be equally divided.

5. The Senate shall choose their other officers, and also a President *pro tempore*, in the absence of the Vice-President, or when he shall exercise the office of President of the United States.

6. The Senate shall have the sole power to try all impeachments; when sitting for that purpose, they shall be on oath, or affirmation. When the President of the United States is tried, the Chief Justice shall preside, and no person shall be convicted without the concurrence of two thirds of the members present.

7. Judgment in cases of impeachment shall not extend farther than to removal from office, and disqualification to hold and enjoy any office of honor, trust, or profit under the United States; but the party convicted shall nevertheless be liable and subject to indictment, trial, judgment and punishment, according to law.

SECTION IV.—*Election of Members.*

1. The times, places, and manner of holding elections for Senators

and Representatives, shall be prescribed in each State by the Legislature thereof; but the Congress may at any time by law make or alter such regulations, except as to the places of choosing Senators.

2. The Congress shall assemble at least once in every. year, and such meeting shall be on the first Monday in December, unless they shall by law appoint a different day.

Section V.—*Powers of each House.*

1. Each House shall be the judge of the elections, returns, and qualifications of its own members, and a majority of each shall constitute a quorum to do business; but a smaller number may adjourn from day to day, and may be authorized to compel the attendance of absent members, in such manner, and under such penalties, as each House may provide.

2. Each House may determine the rules of its proceedings, punish its members for disorderly behavior. and, with the concurrence of two thirds, expel a member.

3. Each House shall keep a journal of its proceedings, and from time to time publish the same, excepting such parts as may in their judgment require secresy; and the yeas and nays of the members of either House on any question shall, at the desire of one fifth of those present, be entered on the journal.

4. Neither House, during the session of Congress, shall, without the consent of the other, adjourn for more than three days, nor to any other place than that in which the two Houses shall be sitting.

Section VI.—*Compensation, Privileges, Etc.*

1. The Senators and Representatives shall receive a compensation for their services, to be ascertained by law, and paid out of the Treasury of the United States. They shall, in all cases, except treason, felony and breach of peace, be privileged from arrest during their attendance at the session of their respective Houses, and in going to and returning from the same; and for any speech or debate in either House, they shall not be questioned in any other place.

2. No Senator or Representative shall, during the time for which he was elected, be appointed to any civil office under the authority of the United States, which shall have been created, or the emoluments whereof shall have been increased during such time; and no person holding any office under the United States, shall be a member of either House during his continuance in office.

Section VII.—*Bills and Resolutions, Etc.*

1. All bills for raising revenue shall originate in the House of Repre-

sentatives: but the Senate may propose, or concur with amendments, as on other bills.

2. Every bill which shall have passed the House of Representatives and the Senate, shall, before it become a law, be presented to the President of the United States; if he approve he shall sign it, but if not he shall return it, with his objections, to that House in which it shall have originated, who shall enter the objections at large on their journal, and proceed to reconsider it. If, after such reconsideration, two thirds of that House shall agree to pass the bill, it shall be sent, together with the objections, to the other House, by which it shall, likewise, be reconsidered; and if approved by two thirds of that House, it shall become a law. But in all such cases the votes of both Houses shall be determined by yeas and nays, and the names of the persons voting for and against the bill shall be entered on the journal of each House respectively. If any bill shall not be returned by the President within ten days (Sundays excepted) after it shall have been presented to him, the same shall be a law in like manner as if he had signed it, unless the Congress by their adjournment prevent its return, in which case it shall not be a law.

3. Every order, resolution, or vote, to which the concurrence of the Senate and House of Representatives may be necessary (except on a question of adjournment,) shall be presented to the President of the United States; and before the same shall take effect, shall be approved by him, or being disapproved by him, shall be repassed by two thirds of the Senate and House of Representatives, according to the rules and limitations prescribed in the case of a bill.

SECTION VIII.—*Powers of Congress.*

1. The Congress shall have power to lay and collect taxes, duties, imposts and excises to pay the debts and provide for the common defense and general welfare of the United States; but all duties, imposts and excises, shall be uniform throughout the United States.

2. To borrow money on the credit of the United States.

3. To regulate commerce with foreign nations, and among the several States, and with the Indian tribes.

4. To establish a uniform rule of naturalization, and uniform laws on the subject of bankruptcies throughout the United States.

5. To coin money, regulate the value thereof, and of foreign coin, and fix the standard of weights and measures.

6. To provide for the punishment of counterfeiting the securities and current coin of the United States.

7. To establish post-offices and post roads.

8. To promote the progress of science and useful arts, by securing for limited times to authors and inventors the exclusive right to their respective writings and discoveries.

9. To constitute tribunals inferior to the Supreme Court.

10. To define and punish piracies and felonies committed on the high seas, and offenses against the law of nations.

11. To declare war, grant letters of marque and reprisal, and make rules concerning captures on land and water.

12. To raise and support armies, but no appropriation of money to that use shall bo for a longer term than two years.

13. To provide and maintain a navy.

14. To make rules for the government and regulation of the land and naval forces.

15. To provide for calling forth the militia to execute the laws of the Union, suppress insurrections and repel invasions.

16. To provide for organizing, arming and disciplining the militia, and for governing such part of them as may be employed in the service of the United States, reserving to the States, respectively, the appointment of the officers and the authority of training the militia according to the discipline prescribed by Congress.

17. To exercise exclusive legislation, in all cases whatsoever, over such district (not exceeding ten miles square) as may, by cession of particular States, and the acceptance of Congress, become the seat of the Government of the United States, and to exercise like authority over all places purchased by the consent of the Legislature of the State in which the same shall be, for the erection of forts, magazines, arsenals, dock-yards, and other needful buildings; and,

18. To make all laws which shall be necessary and proper for carrying into execution the foregoing powers, and all other powers vested by this Constitution in the Government of the United States, or in any department or office thereof.

SECTION IX.—*Prohibitions and Privileges.*

1. The migration or importation of such persons as any of the States now existing shall think proper to admit, shall not be prohibited by the Congress prior to the year 1808, but a tax or duty may be imposed on such importation, not exceeding ten dollars on each person.

2. The privilege of the writ of *Habeas Corpus* shall not be suspended, unless when in cases of rebellion or invasion the public safety may require it.

3. No bill of attainder or expost facto law shall be passed.

4. No capitation or other direct tax shall be laid, unless in proportion to the census or enumeration herein before directed to be taken.

5. No tax or duty shall be laid on articles exported from any State.

6. No preference shall be given by any regulation of commerce or revenue to the ports of one State over those of another; nor shall vessels

bound to, or from, one State, be obliged to enter, clear, or pay duties in another.

7. No money shall be drawn from the Treasury but in consequence of appropriation made by law ; and a regular statement and account of the receipts and expenditures of all public money shall be published from time to time.

8. No title of nobility shall be granted by the United States ; and no person holding any office of profit or trust under them, shall, without the consent of the Congress, accept of any present, emolument, office, or title of any kind whatever, from any king, prince, or foreign state.

SECTION X.—*State Restrictions.*

1. No State shall enter into any treaty, alliance, or confederation ; grant letters of marque and reprisal, coin money, emit bills of credit, make any thing but gold and silver coin a tender in payment of debts, pass any bill of attainder, ex post facto law, or law impairing the obligation of contracts, or grant any title of nobility.

2. No State shall, without the consent of the Congress, lay any imposts or duties on imports or exports, except what may be absolutely necessary for executing its inspection laws, and the net produce of all duties and imposts, laid by any State on imports or exports, shall be for the use of the Treasury of the United States ; and all such laws shall be subject to the revision and control of the Congress.

3. No State shall, without the consent of Congress, lay any duty on tonage, keep troops, or ships of war in time of peace, enter into any agreement or compact with another State, or with a foreign power, or engage in war, unless actually invaded, or in such imminent danger as will not admit of delay.

ARTICLE II.—PRESIDENT.

1. The executive power shall be vested in a President of the United States of America. He shall hold his office during the term of four years, and together with the Vice-President, chosen for the same term, be elected as follows :

2. Each State shall appoint, in such manner as the Legislature thereof may direct, a number of Electors, equal to the whole number of Senators and Representatives to which the State may be entitled in the Congress; but no Senator or Representative, or person holding an office of trust or profit under the United States, shall be appointed an Elector.

3. [The electors shall meet in their respective States, and vote by ballot for two persons, of whom one, at least, shall not be an inhabitant of the same State with themselves. And they shall make a list of all the persons voted for, and of the number of votes for each ; which list they

shall sign and certify, and transmit sealed to the seat of the Government of the United States, directed to the President of the Senate. The President of the Senate shall, in the presence of the Senate and House of Representatives, open all the certificates, and the votes shall then be counted. The person having the greatest number of votes shall be the President, if such number be a majority of the whole number of electors appointed; and if there be more than one who have such majority, and have an equal number of votes, then the House of Representatives shall immediately choose by ballot one of them for President; and if no person have a majority, then from the five highest on the list the said House shall in like manner choose the President. But in choosing the President, the votes shall be taken by States, the representation from each State having one vote; a quorum for this purpose shall consist of a member or members from two thirds of the States, and a majority of all the States shall be necessary to a choice. In every case, after the choice of the President, the person having the greatest number of votes of the electors shall be the Vice-President. But if there should remain two or more who have equal votes, the Senate shall choose from them by ballot the Vice-President.]

[*This clause altogether altered and supplied by the XII. Amendment.*]

4. The Congress may determine the time of choosing the Electors, and the day on which they shall give their votes, which day shall be the same throughout the United States.

5. No person, except a natural born citizen, or a citizen of the United States at the time of the adoption of this Constitution, shall be eligible to the office of President; neither shall any person be eligible to that office who shall not have attained to the age of thirty-five years, and been fourteen years a resident within the United States.

6. In case of the removal of the President from office, or of his death, resignation, or inability to discharge the powers and duties of the said office, the same shall devolve on the Vice-President, and the Congress may by law provide for the case of removal, death, resignation, or inability both of the President and Vice-President, declaring what officer shall then act as President, and such officer shall act accordingly, until the disability be removed, or a President shall be elected.

7. The President shall, at stated times, receive for his services a compensation, which shall neither be increased nor diminished during the period for which he shall have been elected, and he shall not receive within that period any other emolument from the United States or any of them.

8. Before he enter on the execution of his office, he shall take the following oath or affirmation:

"I do solemnly swear (or affirm) that I will faithfully execute the office of President of the United States, and will, to the best of my ability, preserve, protect, and defend the Constitution of the United States."

SECTION II.—*Powers of the President.*

1. The President shall be commander-in-chief of the army and navy of the United States, and of the militia of the several States, when called into the actual service of the United States; he may require the opinion, in writing, of the principal officer in each of the executive departments upon any subject relating to the duties of their respective offices, and he shall have power to grant reprieves and pardons for offenses against the United States, except in cases of impeachment.

2. He shall have power, by and with the advice and consent of the Senate, to make treaties, provided two thirds of the Senators present concur; and he shall nominate, and by and with the advice and consent of the Senate, shall appoint ambassadors, other public ministers and consuls, judges of the Supreme Court, and all other officers of the United States whose appointments are not herein otherwise provided for, and which shall be established by law; but the Congress may by law vest the appointment of such inferior officers as they think proper in the President alone, in the courts of law, or in the heads of departments.

3. The President shall have power to fill up all vacancies that may happen during the recess of the Senate, by granting commissions which shall expire at the end of their next session.

SECTION III.—*Duties of the President.*

1. He shall from time to time give to the Congress information of the state of the Union, and recommend to their consideration such measures as he shall judge necessary and expedient; he may, on extraordinary occasions, convene both Houses, or either of them, and, in case of disagreement between them, with respect to the time of adjournment, he may adjourn them to such time as he shall think proper; he shall receive ambassadors and other public ministers; he shall take care that the laws be faithfully executed, and shall commission all the officers of the United States.

SECTION IV.—*Impeachment of Officers.*

1. The President, Vice-President, and all civil officers of the United States, shall be removed from office on impeachment for, and conviction of, treason, bribery, or other high crimes and misdemeanors.

ARTICLE III.—JUDICIARY.

SECTION I.—*Courts—Judges.*

1. The judicial power of the United States shall be vested in one Supreme Court, and in such inferior courts as the Congress may from

time to time ordain and establish. The judges, both of the Supreme and inferior courts, shall hold their offices during good behavior, and shall, at stated times, receive for their services a compensation which shall not be diminished during their continuance in office.

SECTION II.—*Judicial Powers—Civil—Criminal.*

1. The judicial power shall extend to all cases in law and equity, arising under this Constitution, the laws of the United States, and treaties made, or which shall be made under their authority; to all cases affecting ambassadors, other public ministers, and consuls; to all cases of admiralty and maritime jurisdiction; to controversies to which the United States shall be a party; to controversies between two or more States—between a State and the citizens of another State—between citizens of different States—between citizens of the same State claiming lands under grants of different States—and between a State, or the citizens thereof, and foreign States, citizens or subjects.

2. In all cases affecting ambassadors, other public ministers and consuls, and those in which a State shall be a party, the Supreme Court shall have original jurisdiction. In all the other cases before mentioned, the Supreme Court shall have appellate jurisdiction, both as to the law and fact, with such exceptions, and under such regulations as the Congress shall make.

3. The trial of all crimes, except in cases of impeachment, shall be by jury; and such trial shall be held in the State where the said crimes shall have been committed; but when not committed within any State, the trial shall be at such place or places as the Congress may by law have directed.

SECTION III.—*Treason.*

1. Treason against the United States shall consist only in levying war against them, or in adhering to their enemies, giving them aid and comfort. No person shall be convicted of treason unless on the testimony of two witnesses to the same overt act, or on confession in open court.

2. The Congress shall have power to declare the punishment of treason, but no attainder of treason shall work corruption of blood, or forfeiture, except during the life of the person attained.

ARTICLE IV.—STATE RIGHTS.

SECTION I.—*Restitution and Privileges.*

1. Full faith and credit shall be given in each State to the public acts, records, and judicial proceedings of every other State. And the Congress may by general laws prescribe the manner in which such acts, records and proceedings shall be proved, and the effect thereof.

SECTION II.—*Privilege of Citizens.*

1. The citizens of each State shall be entitled to all privileges and immunities of citizens in the several States.

2. A person charged in any State with treason, felony, or other crime, who shall flee from justice, and be found in another State, shall on demand of the Executive authority of the State from which he fled, be delivered up, to be removed to the State having jurisdiction of the crime.

3. No person held to service or labor in one State under the laws thereof, escaping into another, shall, in consequence of any law or regulation therein, be discharged from such service or labor, but shall be delivered up on claim of the party to whom such service or labor may be due.

SECTION III.—*New States.*

1. New States may be admitted by the Congress into this Union; but no new State shall be formed or erected within the jurisdiction of any other State; nor any State be formed by the junction of two or more States, or parts of States, without the consent of the Legislatures of the States concerned, as well as of the Congress.

2. The Congress shall have power to dispose of and make all needful rules and regulations respecting the territory or other property belonging to the United States, and nothing in this Constitution shall be so construed as to prejudice any claims of the United States, or of any particular State.

SECTION IV.—*State Governments—Republican.*

1. The United States shall guarantee to every State in this Union a republican form of government, and shall protect each of them against invasion; and on application of the Legislature, or of the Executive (when the Legislature cannot be convened), against domestic violence.

ARTICLE V.—AMENDMENTS.

1. The Congress, whenever two thirds of both Houses shall deem it necessary, shall propose amendments to this Constitution, or, on the application of the Legislatures of two thirds of the several States, shall call a convention for proposing amendments, which, in either case, shall be valid to all intents and purposes, as part of this Constitution when ratified by the Legislatures of three fourths of the several States, or by conventions in three fourths thereof, as the one or the other mode of ratification may be proposed by the Congress; provided that no amendment which may be made prior to the year 1808 shall in any manner affect the first and fourth clauses in the ninth section of the first article; and that no State, without its consent, shall be deprived of its equal suffrage in the Senate.

ARTICLE VI.—Debts.

1. All debts contracted, and engagements entered into, before the adoption of this Constitution, shall be as valid against the United States under this Constitution, as under the confederation.

2. This Constitution, and the laws of the United States which shall be made in pursuance thereof; and all treaties made, or which shall be made, under the authority of the United States, shall be the supreme law of the land; and the judges in every State shall be bound thereby, anything in the Constitution or laws of any State to the contrary notwithstanding.

3. The Senators and Representatives before mentioned, and the members of the several State Legislatures, and all executive and judicial officers, both of the United States and of the several States, shall be bound, by oath or affirmation, to support this Constitution; but no religious test shall ever be required as a qualification to any office or public trust under the United States.

ARTICLE VII.—Ratification.

1. The ratification of the conventions of nine States shall be sufficient for the establishment of this Constitution between the States so ratifying the same.

Done in Convention, by the unanimous consent of the States present, the seventeenth day of September, in the year of our Lord, one thousand seven hundred and eighty-seven, and of the Independence of the United States of America, the Twelfth.

In witness whereof, we have hereunto subscribed our names.

GEORGE WASHINGTON,

ATTEST: *President, and Deputy from Virginia.*

WM. JACKSON, *Secretary.*

AMENDMENTS.

Articles in addition to, and amendment of the Constitution of the United States of America, proposed by Congress, and ratified by the Legislatures of the several States, pursuant to the Fifth article of the original Constitution.

Article I.

Congress shall make no law respecting an establishment of religion, or prohibiting the free exercise thereof; or abridging the freedom of speech, or of the press; or the right of the people peaceably to assemble, and to petition the Government for a redress of grievances.

Article II.

A well regulated militia being necessary to the security of a free State, the right of the people to keep and bear arms shall not be infringed.

Article III.

No soldier shall, in time of peace, be quartered in any house without the consent of the owner, nor in time of war but in a manner to be prescribed by law.

Article IV.

The right of the people to be secure in their persons, houses, papers and effects, against unreasonable searches and seizures, shall not be violated; and no warrants shall issue, but upon probable cause, supported by oath or affirmation, and particularly describing the place to be searched, and the persons or things to be seized.

Article V.

No person shall be held to answer for a capital or otherwise infamous crime, unless on a presentment or indictment of a grand jury, except in cases arising in the land or naval forces, or in the militia when in actual service, in time of war or public danger; nor shall any person be subject, for the same offense, to be twice put in jeopardy of life or limb; nor shall be compelled in any criminal case to be a witness against himself; nor be deprived of life, liberty or property, without due process of law; nor shall private property be taken for public use without just compensation.

Article VI.

In all criminal prosecutions, the accused shall enjoy the right to a speedy and public trial by an impartial jury of the State and district wherein the crime shall have been committed, which district shall have been previously ascertained by law; and to be informed of the nature and cause of the accusation; to be confronted with the witnesses against him; to have compulsory process for obtaining witnesses in his favor; and to have the assistance of counsel for his defense.

Article VII.

In suits at common law, where the value in controversy shall exceed twenty dollars, the right of trial by jury shall be preserved; and no fact, tried by a jury shall be otherwise re-examined in any court of the United States, than according to the rules of the common law.

Article VIII.

Excessive bail shall not be required, nor excessive fines imposed, nor cruel and unusual punishments inflicted.

Article IX.

The enumeration in the Constitution of certain rights shall not be construed to deny or disparage others retained by the people.

Article X.

The powers not delegated to the United States by the Constitution, nor prohibited by it to the States, are reserved to the States respectively, or to the people.

Article XI.

The judicial power of the United States shall not be construed to extend to any suit in law or equity commenced or prosecuted against one of the United States, by citizens of another State, or by citizens or subjects of any foreign State.

Article XII.

The Electors shall meet in their respective States, and vote by ballot for President and Vice-President, one of whom, at least, shall not be an inhabitant of the same State with themselves; they shall name in their ballots the person voted for as President, and in distinct ballots the person voted for as Vice-President, and they shall make distinct lists of all persons voted for as President, and of all persons voted for as Vice-President, and of the number of votes for each, which lists they shall sign and certify, and transmit, sealed, to the seat of the Government of the United States, directed to the President of the Senate; the President of the Senate shall, in presence of the Senate and House of Representatives, open all the certificates, and the votes shall then be counted. The person having the greatest number of votes for President shall be the President, if such number be a majority of the whole number of Electors appointed; and if no person have such majority, then from the persons having the highest numbers, not exceeding three, on the list of those voted for as President, the House of Representatives shall choose immediately, by ballot, the President. But in choosing the President, the votes shall be taken by States, the representation from each State having one vote; a quorum for this purpose shall consist of a member or members from two thirds of the States, and a majority of all the States shall be necessary to a choice. And if the House of Representatives shall not choose a President whenever the right of choice shall devolve upon them, before the fourth day of March next following, then the Vice-President shall act as President, as in case of the death or other constitutional disability of the President.

The person having the greatest number of votes as Vice-President shall be the Vice-President, if such number be a majority of the whole number of Electors appointed, and if no person have a majority, then from the two highest numbers on the list the Senate shall choose the Vice-President; a quorum for the purpose shall consist of two thirds of the whole number of Senators, and a majority of the whole number shall be necessary to a choice.

But no person constitutionally ineligible to the office of President, shall be eligible to that of Vice-President of the United States.

[An article intended as a thirteenth amendment to the Constitution was proposed at the Second Session of the Eleventh Congress, but was not ratified by a sufficient number of States to become valid as a part of the Constitution. It is erroneously given in an edition of the Laws of the United States, published by Bioren and Duane in 1815.]

[NOTE.—The eleventh article of the amendments to the Constitution was proposed at the Second Session of the Third Congress; the twelfth article, at the First Session of the Eighth Congress; and the thirteenth article at the Second Session of the Eleventh Congress.]

Article XIII.

Neither slavery nor involuntary servitude, except as a punishment for crime, whereof the party shall have been duly convicted, shall exist within the United States, or any place subject to their jurisdiction.

Article XIV.

SECTION 1. All persons born or naturalized in the United States, and subject to the jurisdiction thereof, are citizens of the United States, and of the State wherein they reside. No State shall make or enforce any law which shall abridge the privileges or immunities of citizens of the United States; nor shall any State deprive any person of life, liberty, or property, without due process of law, nor deny to any person within its jurisdiction the equal protection of the laws.

SEC. 2. Representatives shall be apportioned among the several States according to their respective numbers, counting the whole number of persons in each State, excluding Indians not taxed. But when the right to vote at any election for the choice of electors for President and

Vice-President of the United States, representatives in Congress, the executive and judicial officers of a State, or the members of the legislature thereof, is denied to any of the male inhabitants of such State, being twenty-one years of age, and citizens of the United States, or in any way abridged, except for participation in rebellion or other crime, the basis of representation therein shall be reduced in the proportion which the number of such male citizens shall bear to the whole number of male citizens twenty-one years of age in such State.

SEC. 3. No person shall be a Senator or Representative in Congress, or elector of President and Vice-President, or hold any office, civil or military, under the United States, or under any State, who, having previously taken an oath, as a member of Congress, or as an officer of the United States, or as a member of any State legislature, or as an executive or judicial officer of any State, to support the Constitution of the United States, shall have engaged in insurrection or rebellion against the same, or given aid or comfort to the enemies thereof. But Congress may, by a vote of two thirds of each House, remove such disability.

SEC. 4. The validity of the public debt of the United States, authorized by law, including debts incurred for payment of pensions and bounties for services in suppressing insurrection or rebellion, shall not be questioned. But neither the United States nor any State shall assume or pay any debt or obligation incurred in aid of insurrection or rebellion against the United States, or any claim for the loss or emancipation of any slave; but all such debts, obligations, and claims shall be held illegal and void.

SEC. 5. The Congress shall have power to enforce, by appropriate legislation, the provisions of this article.

Article XV.

SECTION 1. The right of citizens of the United States to vote shall not be denied or abridged by the United States, or by any State, on account of race or color, or previous condition of servitude.

SEC. 2. The Congress shall have power to enforce this article by appropriate legislation.

TABLE OF CONTENTS.

The Census :

www.ingramcontent.com/pod-product-compliance
Lightning Source LLC
Chambersburg PA
CBHW031443280326
41927CB00038B/1572